WOMAN IN IRISH LEGEND, LIFE AND LITERATURE

Irish Literary Studies
General Editor
Colin Smythe

IRISH LITERARY STUDIES

Woman in Irish Legend, Life and Literature

edited by

S. F. Gallagher

Irish Literary Studies 14

1983
COLIN SMYTHE
Gerrards Cross, Bucks.

BARNES AND NOBLE BOOKS
Totowa, New Jersey

First published in 1983 by Colin Smythe Limited
P.O. Box 6, Gerrards Cross, Buckinghamshire

British Library Cataloguing in Publication Data
Woman in Irish legend, life and literature.—(Irish
literary studies, ISSN 0140-895X; 14)
1. English literature—Irish authors—History and
criticism.   2. Women in literature
I. Gallagher, S.F.   II. Series
820.8'0354   PR8835
ISBN 0-86140-159-X

Published in Canada by the Canadian Association for Irish Studies
as Volume VIII Number 2 of *The Canadian Journal of Irish Studies*,
Department of English, University of British Columbia, Vancouver, B.C.

First published in the U.S.A. in 1983 by Barnes and Noble Books,
Totowa, New Jersey 07502

Library of Congress Cataloging in Publication Data
Main entry under title:

Woman in Irish Legend, life, and literature.

(Irish literary studies, ISSN 0140-895X; 14)
"Essays . . . presented to the fourteenth international
seminar of the Canadian Association for Irish Studies
at Trent University, Peterborough, Ontario, March 1981"—
Introd.
Includes index.
1. Women in literature—Addresses, essays, lectures.
2. English literature—Irish authors—History and
criticism—Addresses, essays, lectures.   3. Irish
literature—History and criticism—Addresses, essays,
lectures.   I. Gallagher, S. F.   II. Canadian Association
for Irish Studies, International Seminar (14th: 1981: Trent University)
PR8723.W6W65 1983   820'.9'9287   82-22792
ISBN 0-389-20361-0 (Barnes and Noble Books)

Printed in Great Britain

Typeset by Inforum Ltd., Portsmouth
and printed and bound by Billing & Sons Ltd.,
Worcester and London

CONTENTS

This volume is published in Canada as Volume 8 number 2 of the *Canadian Journal of Irish Studies* with the aid of the Social Sciences and Humanities Research Council of Canada.

INTRODUCTION

With the exception of Maire Cruise O'Brien's, the essays in this book were first presented to the fourteenth international seminar of the Canadian Association for Irish Studies at Trent University, Peterborough, Ontario, March 1981, on 'Woman in Irish Legend, Life and Literature'. Other Seminar '81 papers (by Liam de Paor, Anne Dooley, Denis Donoghue, Margaret MacCurtain and Ninian Mellamphy) unfortunately were unavailable for publication here.

Though one cannot recapture the atmosphere of their original context, I have tried, in editing these papers, not to tamper with whatever colloquial flavour their authors thought fit to preserve. Certain of the conference's highlights, however, defy translation: Lorna Reynolds's exuberant keynote lecture punctuated by such mischievous asides as 'Never mind me: the *scholarly* papers come later'; a spontaneous and erudite debate on different forms of the *caoineadh* (lament); an exquisite concert, 'The Irish Woman in Song and Music', by Nóirín Ní Riain (vocalist) and Mícháel Ó'Súilleabháin (piano and harpsichord); an evening *céilidhe*, sponsored by the Peterborough Canadian Irish Club to demonstrate local traditions of Irish song, music and dance; and, at the concluding banquet, the standing ovation evoked by Margaret Laurence's brief but eloquent response (see *Appendix*) to Eugene Benson's graceful toast to Canada.

Neither the seminar nor this collection of essays could hope to cover adequately the vast terrain conjured up by their common theme. (Perhaps not even the cloak of St. Bridget, to which Lorna Reynolds alludes, could have done that.) Curiously, however – and presumably without conscious collaboration – several of the writers here furnish individual insights whose cumulative effect is to suggest, or hint, potential patterns of chronological or generic coherence. Conversely, one encounters also a delightful diversity of assumptions or conclusions that occasionally approaches outright contradiction: granted, no novelty in Irish legend, literature or life. To savour such qualities, it may be advisable to read these essays in

7

sequence, but however one takes them, they offer an intriguing blend of stimulation and provocation.

The CAIS could scarcely continue its seminars, or publish the papers thereof, without the regular moral and financial support of the Social Sciences and Humanities Research Council of Canada and the Department of Foreign Affairs (Cultural Relations) of the Government of Ireland. To both bodies, and to many others who helped with Seminar '81 or this publication, we are indeed grateful.

Presuming editorial privilege, I dedicate this volume (primarily the work of others) to those who inspired it, the women of Ireland; especially to Eileen, Eithne, Maureen, Nora and Noreen.

S.F. Gallagher,
Trent University,
Peterborough, Ontario.

IRISH WOMEN IN LEGEND, LITERATURE AND LIFE

LORNA REYNOLDS

I have a vast subject to put before you in a short time, so I am going to simplify things for myself by being personal and begin by recalling some memories of my childhood. One of the stories I liked best to hear about my father was how he was once on a train journey home on a side-branch of the railway which used to stop at a halt – not a station proper, but a rural halt, called Brosna, provided for the convenience of an important family in the neighbourhood – and there, on this occasion, the only passenger to alight was a beautiful girl. 'By Jove,' said the young English officer who was in the carriage with my father, 'there goes a stunning girl; such hair, such a complexion, such a sweet expression, what I call a real Irish colleen. Who is she, do you know?' 'I don't know,' said my father, 'but I'll ask the guard.' So he called the guard and asked who the Irish colleen was. 'That' said the guard, 'is the Lady Flora Hastings, daughter of the Earl of Huntingdon – Sir.'

My second memory is of May-time, and my becoming aware, for the first time, of the glorious heavy-scented blossom the the hawthorn. I was visiting my grandmother, and, 'mad about flowers' as I was, I broke off a great branch of the foamy white flowers and brought it into the house. My aunt, when she saw what I had in my hands, went white as a sheet, snatched it from me and threw it out the back door as far as she could from the house. 'Never bring hawthorn into the house, child,' she said, 'it's very unlucky.'

I thought her very silly – how could bringing flowers of any kind into the house be unlucky? – and it wasn't until many years afterwards that I discovered in Robert Graves's *The White Goddess* the reason for my aunt's fear of the hawthorn blossom. It was a millennia-old fear: the hawthorn had been sacred to the bronze-age deity, called the White Goddess by Robert Graves, otherwise known as the great Mother Goddess, Lady of the harvest, of the barley, Goddess of germination and growth, love and battle, death and divination, the Moon Goddess, Ceridwen to the Welsh, Cardea to the Romans, Isis to the Egyptians, great Dana of the Tuatha dé Danaans to the Irish. Nobody would tell me, when I was a child, why

11

the hawthorn was unlucky, but all were agreed that it was. The reason was that the flower was sacred to the White Goddess and she would kill the children of the house that desecrated her flowers.

We have here a prohibition persisting for about twelve hundred generations, condemned by Christianity but unaffected by it, once part of a body of religious belief, evidence of a matriarchal culture still exercising a hold over women's feelings, for men seemed rather indifferent in the matter. Ireland had once participated in that bronze-age culture in which the dominant divinity had been female, the great, all-powerful Mother Goddess. It seems to me that this is something to remember if we are properly to consider Irish women in Legend, Literature and Life.

My first memory serves to illustrate the sentimental, nineteenth-century notion of the Irish colleen, the gentle modest creature, with the shawl over her head and the limpid, trusting eyes, a notion perpetuated until quite recently by the figure on our pound notes. This colleen was as artificial as the colleen of my father's story: she was Lady Lavery, got up in rural fancy dress. Literary echoes of the colleen continued to crop up for a long time, sometimes with a nice irony. In *The Ante-Room* (1934) Kate O'Brien has the visiting London cancer specialist imagine that the two daughters of the house might offer some amatory titillation:

Sir Godfrey Bartlett-Crowe was a connoisseur of women up and down the social scale but he had never met an Irish Colleen. Amusedly in the train he had wondered about the species, shy and wild, no doubt – perhaps even barefoot – and in need of masterly coaxing. He had an idea his technique would serve. Perhaps a little teasing – a playful reproduction of their quaint brogue.
These ladies were not shy and wild, and though they had a brogue, Sir Godfrey felt that its movements were too subtle for immediate imitation. In any case – that obviously would not be the way to please, or to be understood. He bowed in rather excited courtesy over Marie-Rose's beautiful and mondaine hand.

The stereotype of an older Irish woman – the benign, silver-haired lady, framed in an archway of roses – is as false and misleading as that of the colleen. The truth is that the Irish women of legend, literature and life are women of formidable character and tenacious will, if not always of distinguished ancestry. Even the saints among them, such as St. Bridget, are not far removed from their prototype, the White Goddess, and can punish severely those who anger them, as well as take a mile when they are given an inch:

St. Bridget was promised as much land as her cloak could cover; she dropped it on the ground and it spread and spread to cover as many acres as she wanted.

The earliest group of Irish stories, the stories of the Red Branch, suggest to me that they deal with a time when a matriarchal organization of society had not long yielded to a patriarchal one. Of the prime hero, Cuchulainn, we hear that he had to go for his final polishing in arms to a woman warrior, Scathach of Scotland, and that he only overcame her rival, the Amazonian Princess Aoife, by a trick. It was from Scathach that he got the gae-bolg, the weapon which rendered him invincible and saved him from defeat by his unknown son, Connla, and by his friend and foster brother, Ferdia. Cuchulainn is a tragic figure and tragic figures cluster around him, and I shall take one of my legendary women from the Red Branch stories, the story of the sons of Usnach. But first I shall deal with something lighter, with Queen Maeve of Connacht, who started the war described in the *Táin Bó Cuailgne*.

The *Táin* is, I suggest, a comic epic, and Queen Maeve is the heroine of the comedy. She fails to get what she wants, the Brown Bull, but neither does her husband keep his White Bull, because at the end of the *Táin*, the Brown Bull, before dying himself, makes mincemeat of the White Bull and leaves pieces of him scattered about here, there and everywhere. The epic ends, as all comedies do, in compromise and a settlement: Maeve makes peace with the Ulstermen. She is depicted as a masterful, boastful, wilful, power-loving, uninhibited woman, who regards herself as the equal of any man, and one who must be seen to be the equal. Hence the battle for the Brown Bull which, once added to her possessions, will make them exactly equal to her husband's. She seems to me a mixture of Chaucer's Wife of Bath and Harry Percy of Shakespeare's *Henry IV*, he who would 'pluck bright honour from the pale-faced moon'.

The *Táin* begins with a quarrel between Maeve and her husband in which he tries to devalue her as a person and reduce her to the status of a mere wife, a weak woman in need of a man's protection. Maeve will have none of this. 'Today thou art better than the day I married thee', says Ailell to her in the famous opening 'pillow-talk'. 'I was good before ever I had to do with thee', she retorts. 'How well we never heard nor ever knew that', says Ailell, 'but merely that thou didst trust to female women means while enemies of the borders . . . did violently lift from thee thy plunder and thy prey.' 'No, I was the daughter of a king', the queen replies – and goes on to list her father's descent; her own position as the best and haughtiest of his six daughters, to whom he gave a province to rule; the various suitors that came looking for her hand; and the conditions she had laid down as requirements in a suitor, above all the requirement that he should not be jealous: 'for I never had one man without another waiting in his shadow'. She sets herself up as a standard – the man must measure up to her, and she lets Ailell know that he never was, and is not now, the only pebble on the beach.

This angry altercation leads to the enumeration of the goods of each, and because Ailell had a white bull among his herds that she cannot equal, the war for the brown bull begins. In the war it is Maeve who stands out and it is she who gives the orders. Her husband drops out of sight. It is she who cajoles various warriors, including Ferdia, to engage in single combat with Cuchulainn; and the blame for defeat is laid at her door by Fergus Mac Rí. It was the result of – to use Thomas Kinsella's words – 'following the rump of a misguiding woman'. There is something very familiar in all this, is there not? The woman denigrated, the woman asserting herself, and the woman blamed. But it is the personality of the woman, not of her husband, that is stamped on the story, and it is she who lives on in legend and has given her name to the landscape of Sligo.

Maeve patched things up with the Ulstermen and survived her war. She is, as I have said, the heroine of a comedy, but a figure obviously not far removed from the great Mother-Goddess. I turn now to a tragic heroine who did not survive; to Deirdre of *The Sons of Usnach* from the same Red Branch cycle. I think here too we have an illustration of a change from one kind of society to another. Deirdre is in a position, at the beginning of the story, the very reverse of that obtaining in a matriarchal society. She had been chosen, pre-selected, reared in isolation, to be the future sexual partner of the King, Conchubhar MacNessa. She is given no choice in the matter, no more than if she were a mare, or a hound, or any other chattel of the king's. But her character is not in accord with such a passive role. She is no fit subject for a sexual plaything and she asserts her right, as a human being, to love and be loved. She is the leading figure in the drama, clear-headed, single-minded, decisive and brave as any young man, and ready to defy the king, as none of them are. So, when she chooses Naoise, with his raven-black, red and white beauty, she had to put him under *geasa* before he will run away with her: he and she, with his two brothers, lead a happy life in Scotland until the treacherous, alluring messages from the king coax him back to Ireland and the old *camaraderie* in arms. Naoise is torn between the two worlds, of service to the goddess and loyalty to the king, who now had all the power. The two worlds come into collision, and it is the new world of masculine 'solidarity' that wins. Deirdre does not want to return: her intuition tells her how dangerous it would be:

'Do you know of any great want that lies upon you?' asks Conchubhar at the great feast that he gives for the notables of the province. 'We do not, O High King,' say they. 'But I know, O Warriors,' saith he, 'the great want that we have, to wit, that the three lights of Valour of the Gael, the three sons of Usnach, Naoise, Ainle and Aidan should be separated from us on account of any woman in the world.'

Here we have the new masculine society, the 'boys' objecting to the disruption by any woman of their closed circle; and Naoise, when put to the test, is not proof against its attractions. In vain, Deirdre, who is as wise as she is beautiful, warns him against accepting Conchubhar's invitation: in vain, she points out to him the import of every omnious development on the way back. He sets aside her warnings as feminine nonsense, and as a result the sons of Usnach and Deirdre go to their graves.

But there is something more to this tragic tale – laden as it is with dramatic irony – than a story arising from the transition between one culture and another. I have puzzled long over the imaginative pressure behind this story. It is a love story – of course. It is a tragic love story – yes. But there are other tragic love stories that do not awaken quite such repercussions in the mind. Could it be, I ask myself, that the story of Deirdre and Naoise is a prototype? That love between the sexes of this romantic kind could emerge only in a society where women could be disposed of like chattels, and that the true lover could be seen as a deliverer from and protector against other men who would use women and wrong them in the most fundamental way? I suggested on another occasion, at Sligo, in 1976, that Deirdre should not be regarded as the Helen of the Gael but rather as an Andromeda figure, with Conchubhar as the dragon and Naoise as Perseus. Naoise here, however, falls into the snares of the dragon, and both he and Deirdre perish. He tries to compromise but achieves nothing by it. Deirdre holds firm, and dies with her love intact. And this remains true whether we take the ending to be her death on Naoise's body, or the older version where she lives in misery for a year with Conchubhar and then dashes her brains out rather than be handed over to Eoghan Dubhtact.

I am rather inclined to think my third illustration is another prototype. It is the story of Liadán and Cuirthir, from the seventh century A.D., Liadán was a fully fledged woman poet, an ollamh, or professor of poetry, with her train of student poets, in the habit of making the customary circuit of visits to the houses of the great. Once on such a visit to Connacht she met the man poet, Cuirithir, and they fell in love with each other. So, he proposed marriage, suggesting, as an added inducement, no doubt, that a son born to them would surely be famous beyond imagination. Liadán, however, could not interrupt her programme of visits and her professional duties, so she said, 'Meet me later at Corkaguiney and I will go with you'. But the more she thought about it the less she liked the idea. Her destiny, she considered, was to be a poet, not to give birth to a poet. And why was Cuirithir thinking like that? Why was he not content with her company, both of them poets as they were? Yet she loved Cuirithir with all her heart.

She had promised to go with him and intended to keep her promise, but because she realized that marriage would be the death of her as a poet and would spoil the nature of the bond between them, she took the desperate step of making a solemn vow of chastity which there could be no breaking. When he came to meet her as arranged, she went with him but would not marry him nor sleep with him. Bewildered by this and overcome with grief, Cuirithir took a similar vow of chastity, and they both decided to adopt the religious life under the severe St. Cummine. St. Cummine gave Cuirithir the choice of seeing Liadán without talking to her, or talking to her without seeing her, and being a poet, he naturally chose to talk to her. But gradually he was worn down by the exquisite torment of his position and tried to persuade St. Cummine to relax the austerity of his rule. St. Cummine became very angry and banished Cuirithir from the monastic settlement. Furious in his turn, Cuirithir renounced the attempt to live in loving chastity, and wandering off, became a pilgrim. Liadán soon afterwards died of remorse.

This is a most touching, pitiful story: Liadán torn between her fidelity to her vocation as a poet and her love as a woman for Cuirithir, and Cuirithir himself unable to bear the strain of living at once near and far from his beloved. It is interesting, too, in so far as it shows Irish society so long ago accepting the fact that women as well as men could be born with artistic gifts and allowing them to develop these gifts. In this instance it is the man who first breaks under the strain and renounces love. But the woman dies, proving the truth of the Irish triad, that it is death to be a poet, to love a poet, or to mock a poet.

It will not have escaped your notice that the shrinking violet, the Irish colleen, is not to be found in these stories from Irish legend. I turn now to Irish literature, and I take my first example from Carleton's *The Black Prophet*. From a social point of view, one might, I suppose, call the daughter of the black Prophet, Sarah McGowan, a colleen, but psychologically she is far from one. She is, in fact, a brilliantly original creation and might be described as an example of the noble savage in female form, beautiful with the same type of beauty as Naoise – a raven-black, ivory, rose-red beauty. She is absolutely undisciplined, far beyond the control of her father, or her stepmother, and will fight like a tigress if her temper is roused, and it can be roused by a trifle. Yet she is a girl of innate nobility, incapable of lying, spontaneously generous, decisive and energetic. She is tragic in the absolutism of her temperament and will sacrifice herself without hesitation if once her devotion has been given. In fact, Sarah is only as fierce and intractable as she is, we gradually find out, because her capacity for love has not been met and answered. Her naive and total – and misplaced – love for Condy Dalton, who loves, the reader knows, the gentle Mave O'Sullivan, is as touching as it is absurd: she is incapable of subterfuge or pretence and cannot even attempt to hide her feelings. At one moment her jealousy will lead her to agree to help her father in his wicked plans against Mave O'Sullivan; at the next she repents, and, though gravely ill with fever, takes the place of Mave in the attempted abduction scene. She may be said to die from want of love, because her newly discovered mother cannot respond in kind to her ecstatic expressions of love. There is a great deal of melodrama in *The Black Prophet*, but anything melodramatic in the behaviour of Sarah is made psychologically credible by the circumstances of her life. We, the readers, however, do not understand this until we have advanced some way in the novel, and our first impression of her is that of a beautiful, murderous virago. Was there ever a more extraordinary scene than the opening one? Sarah and her stepmother fly at each other in rage, and, the older woman threatening to get the better of her, Sarah seizes an old knife and makes a stab at the heart of her stepmother, 'with an exulting vehemence of vengeance that resembled the growlings which a savage beast makes when springing on its prey'.

If we compare this scene with the last one in the book, we see the range of feeling with which Carleton has endowed the personality of the girl: the tigress is now a lamb, literally sinking into death, because her mother's response to her rapturous welcome is so cool and restrained. In fact the final impression we have is that Sarah is so strange and so wonderful a creation that she must have been modelled on a real person, that nobody could have invented a character of such extremes, with so fine a sensibility, so ruthless a will, so undisciplined a temper and such impetuous generosity.

I move now to the end of the nineteenth century for my second illustration from literature, first recalling for you that in Irish literature in the Irish language the Hag plays a conspicuous part: to accept this we have only to think of the Hag of Beare, the Hag of Battle, the Washer at the Ford, the Hag with the Money, the Hag in the Blanket, and, later on, the Hag who turns into a beautiful young woman, a version of which we all know from Yeats's *Cathleen Ni Houlihan*. I find that the Hag surfaces unexpectedly in Irish literature in the English language. If one reads the stories of Somerville and Ross in *The Irish R.M. Complete*, one gets an impressionistic picture of a whole society, of Irish rural society at the turn of the last century, a time of comparative prosperity in Ireland. It seems to me that the most outstanding creation in this collection is old Mrs. Knox, Flurry Knox's grandmother. Mrs. Knox, like the classic hag, looks one thing but is quite another. In appearance, we are told by Major Yeates, the long-suffering narrator of the tales, Mrs. Knox looks as if 'she had robbed a scarecrow', but her dingy shawls are held together by diamond brooches and on her grubby paw she wears a magnificent ring: she is never seen without distinguishing head-gear, a 'massive purple bonnet' nodding above her fine-boned face. This diamond-decked scarecrow is mistress of every situation: she is the only person whom her grandson, Flurry, considers worthy of his steel and for whom he never makes allowances on the grounds of age or sex. For her part, Mrs. Knox is endowed with a wonderful vitality: she is presented in many an encounter and she can out-talk, out-face and out-manoeuvre everybody. She quotes Virgil to Major Yeates and at the same time screeches an objuration at a being 'whose matted head rose suddenly into view as I have seen the head of a Zulu woman peer over a screen'. She treats Major Yeates as if he had been his own grandfather, who had been a dancing-partner of the old lady in her youth, and serves him a dinner in which the elements are as incongruously mixed as they are in herself: 'detestable soup in a splendid old silver tureen that was nearly as dark as Robinson Crusoe's thumb; a perfect salmon, perfectly cooked on a chipped kitchen dish, such cut glass as is not easy to find nowadays – sherry that, as Flurry subsequently remarked, would burn the shell off an egg; and a bottle of port draped in immemorial cobwebs, wan with age, and probably priceless'.

Mrs. Knox figures in many a story as a perfect specimen of an intelligent, self-possessed, indefatigable, power-loving, power-possessing hag, but she has a benevolent side to her, and her sympathies are wide and often on the side of the young. She unexpectedly cackles with laughter when Flurry's plan to steal Trinket's colt from her, with Major Yeates's treacherous help, is laid bare: she helps Flurry to make a runaway marriage with his cousin, Sally Knox, and dispels her mother's objections – or at least sugars them over – by promising to leave Flurry her acres and her diamonds: she keeps silent when the Major makes the disgraceful *faux-pas* of mistaking a brown collie for a fox and sets the hunt astray. She is as vital – and as unpredictable – at eighty as she had been at eighteen.

Vitality and power characterize another creation of the authors and perhaps their greatest, Charlotte Mullen, the heroine, if one may use the word in this context, of *The Real Charlotte*. Charlotte Mullen would seem to be a type of woman new to Irish literature, a kind of middle-class Lady Macbeth, a coarse-grained, ambitious, intelligent woman who can be greasily hypocritical or brutally frank as occasion demands. Soon after the opening of the novel we find her in command of her circumstances, of independent means, having inherited her aunt's property and money, unencumbered, except by her aunt's feebly uttered wish on her death bed to be 'kind to young Francie', her great-niece, and first cousin once removed of Charlotte. We have become acquainted with young Francie Fitzpatrick already and found her growing up in genteel poverty in Dublin, a pretty, pert, high-spirited orphan girl who even as a child attracted the attention of her uncle's friend, Roddy Lambert. Lambert comes from Lismoyle, Charlotte's town, and links together the two worlds of Dublin and the country town. Charlotte has known him for a long time and on him she has settled her cautious but voracious affections.

Ignorant of any connection between Lambert and Francie, Charlotte, in vestigial observance of her aunt's wish, and nursing plans of her own, invites Francie to stay with her in Lismoyle. The stage is now set for the complicated play of the passions of love, ambition, envy and revenge that is to end in tragedy.

Charlotte's plan for Francie is to marry her off to Christopher Dysart, son of Sir Benjamin Dysart, the leading family and chief landlord of the district. But Francie, while continuing to flirt with Lambert, falls hopelessly in love with Gerard Hawkins, a young English officer, on detachment in Lismoyle; and Lambert's infatuation with Francie makes itself more and more indiscreetly obvious, to the point where Charlotte's eyes are opened and she is forced to realize what is going on. From this follows, first, the death of Lambert's wife, persuaded by Charlotte to investigate her husband's papers and left by Charlotte to die when the shock brings on a heart attack; next, the banishment of Francie from Lismoyle and her return to her uncle's house, empty-hearted, for Lambert, doing his own snooping, has found out that Hawkins is engaged to marry a rich Yorkshire girl. Francie finds her uncle and aunt living in Bray in greater poverty than ever; and straitened circumstances are added to a bruised heart and a vacant future. After some months of this existence, crammed into the small house with her vulgar cousins, cold and undernourished, Francie finds her courageous gaiety has worn thin; and when Lambert, now a widower, arrives and offers marriage, she accepts him. This is the ironic result of Charlotte's brutal treatment of his first wife, and, of all possible results, that least to be desired by her.

Francie's second arrival in Lismoyle is something of a triumph for her. For Charlotte, Lambert's second marriage has been a deathly wound and insult. She sets methodically and unscrupulously about destroying them both. She breaks open Lambert's bank-book and finds out that he has been embezzling money from the Dysart estate and she encourages Francie's renewed relations with Hawkins. Charlotte herself by this time has gone up in the world and is living outside Lismoyle in the 'manor-house' of Gurtnamuckla, having engineered the eviction of old and ailing Miss Julia Duffy from house and lands, and forced her, poverty-stricken as she now is, into the workhouse. Francie and Hawkins, riding together, meet the funeral of Miss Duffy; a flapping cloak frightens Francie's horse; she is flung off and killed. The news is shouted up to Charlotte in her potato loft while she is enjoying the exquisite pleasure of letting Lambert know that it was she who told the Dysarts about his embezzlement of their money.

Charlotte may be called a triple murderer, since the deaths of Mrs. Lambert, Francie and Julia Duffy may be laid at her door: she is an agent of destruction, blighting equally those whom she either desires or hates, a sinister, savage woman, instinct with misused power, and not to be deflected from her purposes. This is the real Charlotte – hidden under the guise of jovial, mannish good-fellowship – without moral scruples of any kind, a raw, grabbing egoist. Not an attractive figure but an Irishwoman.

Moral scruples play no part in guiding Charlotte's actions; neither, of course, do they in Sally McGowan's, who acts from untutored instinct. But Sally's baser instincts are off-set by her honesty and generosity: had she received any moral training, she would, the evidence suggests, have been guided by it. Nevertheless, it is a relief now to turn to a heroine whose dilemma arises precisely from moral scruple. I am taking my third example from Kate O'Brien's *The Ante-Room*, the heroine of which is Agnes Mulqueen. The novel was published in 1934, though the setting is the end of the last century: we may take it, I believe, that the moral sensibility with which Agnes is endowed is drawn from the author's own moral world, and that Agnes Mulqueen represents the educated Catholic girl of the Irish middle classes from the end of the last century through the opening decades of the present. Agnes has received a thorough training in Catholic doctrinal and moral teaching. She is represented as not just accepting her religion but as understanding its exactions, responding to its demands and delighting in its ritual. The three days covered by the action of the novel, Hallowe'en, All Saints' and All Souls', always days of special Catholic ceremony and devotion, are more than usually so for Agnes's family on this occasion. The family are making a special triduum of prayer for their mother, who is dying of cancer. Agnes is forced by necessity of going to confession and receiving Holy Communion to confront her moral dilemma. She is in love, truly, she believes, but impossibly, of course, with her brother-in-law, Vincent O'Regan, married to her pretty, frivolous, much-loved sister, Marie-Rose. Her love for Vincent does not in the least shake her faith, nor does it in the least alter her love for Marie-Rose. But for months she has allowed herself to indulge in dreams about him and now feels that she must put an end to this ambiguous spiritual condition. She is the more determined because Vincent and Marie-Rose are expected on a visit, and resolves to make a general confession and be ready to receive Communion with her family. She is comforted and sustained by her honest confession and by the cold assurance of the priest that no earthly love endures. It needs, however, but Vincent's hand laid on her shoulder in love to shatter her lately won composure, make her realize again the strength of her feeling for him and understand that her conflict has only begun.

The remainder of the novel is given up to this conflict. Agnes, in the end, rejects the invitation of her brother-in-law to run away with him, not because she is forbidden by her religion to do so, but because she cannot face the thought of hurting her sister: one kind of love, passionate and unlawful, is held at bay by another kind, familial and sanctioned. We feel, however, that Agnes could never be happy with an unlawful love, that she needs to be able to live in freedom as well as love: at one point she speculates on what it might be like to be free to love Vincent. In fact, Kate O'Brien's heroines are as much in search of freedom as of love; this makes her a novelist with a message for the modern world.

What she gives us in Agnes Mulqueen is a sophisticated heroine, locked in a conflict of nature and moral training; an uneducated, intelligent heroine, a disciplined as well as a beautiful girl; not at all the simple colleen that the visiting London specialist, running true to type, expects to find, shy and wild, in need of masterly coaxing.

I have made my point, I hope. The women in Irish literature are not the stereotypes that the Sir Godfrey Bartlett-Crowes of this world would make of them. Nothing remains for me now but to talk of Irish women in life.

Life! Oh, dear me, yes. What can one usefully say of life, that abstraction which we make of our fleeting moments? Well, one thing I think one can truthfully, if not usefully, say about Irish women and life, is that, given our sad and troubled history, unless Irish women had been extraordinarily resourceful, adaptable and pertinacious, there would have been no Irish life to mention. When one considers the wars and invasions, the battles and sieges, the laying waste and the destruction, the taxing and the tithing, the harassments and the confiscations, the poverty and the starvation, the restraints and the deprivations, the prohibitions and the exactions, the times of Riot, Rebellion and Martial Law, the Penal laws and the Great Famine – and a great deal more besides – the marvel is that children ever got born, let alone reared and educated. One feels that a great many Irish women must have been like that woman of the MacMahons, married to an O'Brien, who when her husband was killed by the Cromwellians, walked the next day from her castle of Leumanay into Limerick and married a Cromwellian soldier, in order to secure her land and property for her infant son, though not many of them could have had the subsequent satisfaction of kicking the second husband over the battlements when he insulted the memory of the first.

And what, I often ask myself, led Margaret O'Kelly to betray her outlawed lover, Daniel O'Keeffe? He was an outlaw who lived near Mallow in County Cork in the time of William III, and she is supposed to have been tempted by the large reward on his head into betraying him to the British. This is the tradition followed by Edward Walsh in his ballad on the subject: imagining O'Keeffe's lament for his lost love and his remorse for having stabbed her to death, he writes:

> Alas! that my loved one
> Her outlaw could injure–
> Alas! that he e'er proved
> Her treason's avenger,
> That his right hand should make thee
> A bed cold and hollow,
> When in death's sleep it laid thee
> Young Máiréad Ní Chealleadh.

But this banal explanation has never satisfied me. I imagine O'Keeffe somehow insulting the beautiful Máiréad – her beauty, by the way, described as the traditional raven-haired, ivory-skinned, bright-cheeked kind – who had many to choose from, and chose the outlaw. She must have been a proud, unworldly girl and he must have stung her to the quick. Such a one as Sally McGowan, whom one can easily imagine insulted by a lover and rushing to avenge herself; and that Máiréad Ní Cealleadh was no long-sighted, calculating plotter is proved by the fact that she kept on her person the paper that gave her game away and led to her death. I do not know whether it is I who am drawn to these bold, passionate women, or that there are so many of them that one cannot avoid lighting on them.

And yet, when I remember my childhood and the times spent in my grandmother's house in the heart of Ireland, the morality that I imbibed there before I knew what was happening was a morality of gentleness and self-control. In ordinary life the crime of all crimes was to hurt another person's feelings. Nobody put it in so many words, but the implication was clear from what was said about clumsy or malicious people who did hurt other people's feelings. Self-control was necessary to preserve one's dignity and not make a show of oneself. I remember once when I was very small, roaring and bawling about something, and being told to stop making a show of myself, that Gertie was laughing at me. Gertie was my grandmother's cat. It was a most effective admonition. I stopped at once. Gertie was the very essence of aloof self-control, living either under or on top of high cupboards. I did not want to be laughed at by her. Of course, as I grew up, and more especially when I found myself in the academic world and gradually discovered what a cut-throat place it was, I realized that gentleness and self-control would not get one far. I reverted to type, I am afraid, and became rather like those bold resolute women I have been telling you about. I became a politician of the academic world, allowed my naturally quick tongue full play, carried the war into the enemy's camp, and acquired the reputation of being a 'terrible woman'. This I was told by a colleague who joined the staff of University College Dublin about that time and was warned against me. 'Beware of Lorna Reynolds,' she was admonished, 'she's a terrible woman and will stop at nothing.' We became very good friends but I never could get out of her who had given her this dire warning: she was a foreigner and no doubt felt that there were unknown quicksands in which she might perish.

It was the remark, I suppose, of someone who supported the establishment of the day: in pursuit of my new political role, I had become chairman of the Junior Staff Association, and, as such, was often summoned to the President's office. The President of the time was Dr. Michael Tierney, well known as a Platonist and educationalist, and one from whom great things had been expected. Well – either we had all been mistaken, or office changed him. He was a charming man to meet socially, and nothing could have been more delightful than to find oneself seated beside him at a dinner party, entertained by a flow of conversation in which erudition and humour were nicely blended. But, as all gradually came to see, he thought that the way to run the academic staff was to treat everybody, especially the junior members, as an extension of his large family, with a mixture of authoritarianism and emotional blackmail. If one dared to disagree with him he was first hurt and then furious, and in his fury he would pound the table and roar at one. I am sure he carefully planned his outbursts of temper, but it so happens that I had a temper that really snapped before I knew what was happening, and, moreover, I was not accustomed to being roared at.

On one such occasion he suddenly wheeled round in his chair and said to me, 'What is all this nonsense about the Junior Staff? I don't know what's wrong with them. Now, take yourself, you, as a single woman, are much better off with what the college gives you, whatever it is, than I am. I have nine mouths to feed.' I, ignoring the illogicality of this and meaning to be objective, said in return, 'I don't think you can argue like that, Dr. Tierney: it depends on a person's responsibilities.' 'No,' he suddenly roared, banging his desk, 'the college is not responsible for your responsibilities.' 'Neither,' I roared back at him, banging his desk on my side, 'is the college responsible for your nine children.'

After that, when I had reported the exchange to my friends eagerly waiting outside, everybody went around saying that Lorna Reynolds – Dr. Reynolds – had discovered that Mrs. Tierney was going to have twins; the nine mouths having registered on my imagination as the nine open little beaks of children and not at all as including himself and his wife.

Perhaps this may seem unduly autobiographical – but when it comes to Irish women and life, what else can one talk about but oneself and one's friends? My generation in University College Dublin was known, as one wit of the day put it, as the 'generation of the hereditary martyrs': we were the children, or nieces and nephews, of the rebels, soldiers and politicians of the 1916 movement. The women we heard speaking at meetings of college societies or at the Contemporary Club, or the Women's Social and Progressive League, were such as Mrs. Hannah Sheehy Skeffington, Mrs. Kettle, Senator Margaret Pearse and Pamela Hinkson, Katherine Tynan's daughter. Any day one might see in the streets of Dublin Maud Gonne McBride and Mrs. Despard, dressed like mourning queens. Among my fellow students were names like Barbara and Donagh MacDonagh, Colum and Maire Gavan Duffy and Betty Kettle. If among them was a young man called Cyril Cusack who was to become famous as an actor, there was a girl called Mary Lavin who was to become yet more famous as a writer; and another called Doreen Murphy who was to become a distinguished pediatrician and devise a diet that would save phenylketonuriac children from brain damage.

In short, the women of my generation and of the preceding generation were more than able to hold their own in a man's world, and I cannot recall a single, simple colleen among them. Perhaps I have said enough to make it clear that the women of Ireland, whether we look for them in legend, literature or life, do not correspond to the stereotypes that have, so mysteriously, developed in the fertile imaginations of men.

THE FEMALE PRINCIPLE IN GAELIC POETRY

MAIRE CRUISE O'BRIEN

Ireland was never part of the Roman Empire; it is only in 432 with the coming of Christianity that she starts to figure at all seriously in European history or that her own records begin to be kept in writing. 432 is of course an arbitrary date: it represents the coming of Patrick. So it is that at this point in time we are presented with the fascinating spectacle of a living society, lasting well into our own era yet still governed by the conventions and customs of the primitive Indo-European way of life. What we know of what the first missionaries found in Ireland seems to confirm with startling clarity the concepts and insights into the life of Mycenean Greece and Minoan Crete, not to speak of Alexander's Macedon, which we find in, say, the novels of Mary Renault. This is perhaps not, after all, so surprising; Miss Renault must certainly have drawn on modern Celtic scholarship when working on her reconstruction of the ancient world.

In pagan Ireland we find a multiplicity of small kingdoms, each comprising a tribal territory ruled over by a quasi-divine King who is hedged around with ritual taboo and privilege. We find a priestly caste who have assumed the sacral functions which in even more archaic times may have been exercised by the King himself. Above all we find the primaeval mother-goddess playing a quintessential part in the structure of society. The King is legitimized only by marriage with the goddess who – by an extension of her function as Mother Earth – is at once the tribe and its territory. In this manifestation she is known as the Sovereignty – almost a technical term.

In many of the Irish sagas and hero-tales we find Kings and champions using their Mother's name in place of a patronymic – Conor Mac Nessa in the Cuchulain saga, for example. Many also figure as sons of divine personages, and are therefore, of course, exogamous; it is tempting to see the society reflected here as matri-centred, with descent in the female line. In the same saga-cycle this is made almost explicit in the figure of Maeve, who is queen of Connacht in her own right and rules with a consort. The promise of her daughter's hand in marriage, which she uses to entice warriors to her service, would seem to carry with it the reversion of the Kingdom. It is generally accepted that Maeve is a euhemerisation of the goddess herself, but if we accept the hypothesis of descent in the female line, she might well be an heiress and perhaps also a priestess, called after the goddess. Her name means intoxication – which recalls the performance of the pythoness at Delphi. Her daughter, Findabar – meaning perhaps 'fair substance' – in turn would be heiress and transmit the sovereignty.

Scholars, however, are slow to accept this possibility, because the texts on which we rely most for our remarkably detailed knowledge of Irish life – both during and before the early Christian era – show a very male-dominated social structure indeed. For example, women are expressly prohibited from owning land. These texts are that famous *corpus* of Irish jurisprudence, the Brehon laws, so called from the Irish word for judge, *brithern*. Gaelic customary law was highly developed and obsessively detailed. It was transmitted orally – apparently with extreme accuracy – from generation to generation of professional jurists; the latter, as with the other learned professions, hived off from the priestly class so as to constitute the *aes dána*, the learned class. These jurists were passionate casuists, conservatives and archaisers, and so tenacious was the system's hold on the Irish consciousness that it continued to function up to Tudor times. In theory it was sacrosanct, an immutable canon with which Christianity itself could not conflict; any modifications or compromises were made silently. When Christianity introduced literacy, the old Gaelic culture was at first hostile – on the ground that the new techniques were destructive of memory and concentration. Ironically, the first to grasp the utility of writing were the lawyers, who, making innovation the servant of archaism, got the laws down in writing in their obscure incantatory form some time about the seventh century. There is not a trace in them of a matri-centred society. Now this, of course, does not mean that no such society ever existed in Gaelic Ireland. It could mean merely that it had been expunged from the record – just as can be postulated for early Greece, for Rome and for the Bible. The actual ritual that acknowledged the fundamental importance of the goddess, the Kingmaking, continued in practice in spite of a prolonged war of attrition directed against it by the new religion. It is a measure of its strength that in direct confrontation the clerics seem to have been the side that lost out, so that opposition was reduced to diplomacy and infiltration. No King could come rightfully to power without going through a form of symbolic marriage with the sovereignty – accompanied by sacrifice and divination – and this remained the case until as late as Elizabethan times. Without these rites the King's reign was impious; the crops would rot in the ground and the cattle die. As for a woman not owning land affecting the functions of the Goddess: who needed to own land if they *were* the land?

The liturgical experts and officiating priests at these inauguration ceremonies were the poets. In Irish their name *fili* is etymologically 'seer', and they were an offshoot, like the jurists, of the priestly caste who themselves correspond to Caesar's druids in Gaul; much of what we know of Gaelic society corresponds to what we know of Celtic societies generally. In spite of, or rather because of, the importance of their politico-religious role they have not always had a good press. The Elizabethans in Ireland feared them and hanged them as witches – also, of course, for sound political reasons. There is a lively and very hostile account of their activities from those times, which has an unexpected bearing on our subject:

The third sort is called Aosdan, which is to say in English, the bards or the riming septs: and these people be very hurtful to the commonweal, for they chiefly maintain the rebels; and further they do cause them that would be true to be rebellious thieves, extortioners, murderers, raveners, yea and worse if it were possible. Their first practice is, if they see any young man descended from the septs of O's and Mac's, who has half a dozen men about him, they will make him a rime wherein they will commend his fathers and his ancestors, numbering how many heads they have cut off, how many towns they have burned, and how many virgins they have deflowered, how many notable murders they have done, and in the end they will compare him to Hannibal or Scipio or Hercules, or some other famous person; wherewithal the poor fool runs mad and thinks it is indeed so.
Then will he gather a rabble of rakehells to him and he must also get a prophet, who shall tell him how he shall speed, as he thinks. Then will he get him lurking to a side of a wood and there he keepeth himself close until morning; and when it is daylight they will go to the poor villages . . . burning the houses and corn and ransacking the poor cottages. They will drive all the kine and plough horses, with all other cattle and drive them away . . . and when he is in a safe place they will fall to the division of the spoil, according to the discretion of the captain.
Now comes the rimer that made the rime, with his rakry [Gaelic: reciter]. The rakry is he that shall utter the rime; and the rimer himself sits by with the captain very proudly. He brings with him also his harper, who plays all the while that the rakry sings the rime. Also he hath his bard, which is a kind of foolish fellow, who must also have a horse given him; the harper must have a new saffron shirt and a mantle and a hackney; and the rakry must have twenty or thirty kine and the rimer himself horse and harness, with a nag to ride on, a silver goblet, a pair of beads of coral, with buttons of silver – and this, with more, they look for to have for destruction of the commonwealth and to the blasphemy of God; and this is the best thing that the rimers cause them to do . . . .

The account goes on to describe the *file* himself – what we might call the 'poet's poet' – the people who have been so stigmatised for being lesser grades of the profession:

> Fillis, which is to say in English, a poet, have great store of cattle and use all the trades of the others with an addition of prophecies. These are great maintainers of witches and other vile matters; to the great blasphemy of God and to great impoverishing of the Commonwealth.[1]

The reader may not perhaps have realised that this fire-brand, this fomenter of sedition, is acting in his *female* capacity – he is a woman and the bride of his patron! We know from Aristotle that the Celts esteemed homosexuality; so also it would appear did the Gaels – at least for ritual purposes. The Irish poet was fully conscious of his supernatural role. When his verse legitimised the ruler the poet *was* the goddess. Earlier custom seems to have required a cruder acting out of the relationship, a simulated copulation with the totem of the tribe; as it might be, with a white mare – Epona, the Gaulish horse-goddess. In the period of classical Irish poetry (c. 1250–1650) this practice had been refined to a convention of romantic attachment between the ruler and the poet, in which the poet plays the female part.

To this convention we owe a whole school of dramatic lyric poetry – ascribed to women, but undoubtedly written by men. It is from such lyrics and from the dialogue of the sagas, which itself is often in verse, that in happier circumstances we might have expected the growth of Irish theatre. The most famous example of this form is a splendid dramatic apologue in which Eochaidh Ó Heoghusa, a late sixteenth-century poet, addresses his patron, Hugh Maguire of Fermanagh. These are the same poet and the same patron who figure in Mangan's version of *O'Hussey's Ode to the Maguire*. In the ode discussed here, O'Hussey speaks in the character of a wife torn between loyalty to an absent husband and the passionate demands of a present lover. We are fortunate in having a superb translation of the poem by Joan Keefe of Berkeley, University of California. She calls her version 'O'Rourke's Wife' and it has been published, or is about to be published, in an anthology of poems by women authors:

O'Rourke's Wife

(The poem is supposed to be addressed to her husband, Hugh O'Rourke, son of Brian, and to her lover Tomás Costello, son of Siurtán.)

Look at these doings, Hugh,
Flower of the highest bough
Green shoot and my strongest prop,
Look at what Tomás has wrought.
Hurry Hugh, look after me
If you are faithful,
Here is the magic knight
Tempting me in whispers.

Mac Brian, believe my words
If you would not lose me,
Help me then, beloved rib,
Reprimand the son of Siurtán.
Tell him, make him comprehend
No poet's needs I pursued,
As a virgin wife from Cara
I am possessed only by you.

Now that he is after me
This honey-moth of learning
No matter what he promises
Do not think he will lure me;
Your opinion, not mine,
That this poet-thief of Ireland
A lion mauling my thin will
Is wrenching my compliance.

If affection confound me
Then, Hugh, understand
By the Hound of Conn
I cannot abandon him
Then coming with enticement
His pleasure unmistakable
Hidden, but not from me
Towards me is directed.

Often he comes beside me
Swooping like a hawk
Through a crowd to grab my heart,
A sorcerer, to me a saint.
As if I were a tinker girl
That he would pleasure
With magic words and evil rhymes
He pleads with me to go with him.

While other men are fighting wars
For victory with O'Neill
He wins by making love
For my envy with a girl.

Then as you, in your shape, Hugh O'Rourke,
He comes smoothly as a dove,
A tame gentle dragon
Casting spells of love.

But with Tomás himself
Without disguise, I lose my sense,
So dear is he to me
My heart is wrested from its place.

Unless you understand
And help me
Dearest love
I am won over
No way can I divide
Myself between you;

Hugh, my soul is in your care
Tomás, my body is enchained.

Now it is clear that Mrs. Keefe thought of this poem as having been written by an actual historical person who was a woman. This is not surprising, as this was what was generally accepted as being so by authorities in this field until about 1955, when a brilliant Irish scholar, Dr. James Carney, editing O'Hussey's poems, realised that O'Hussey himself was the author of this one and not any possible wife of Hugh Maguire's. O'Hussey is simply letting his chief know in terms as forceful as he can muster that – if Maguire does not pay him better – he will leave him for another patron who is already making offers for him. The key-word is *poet-thief*: this does not mean a thief who is a poet, it means a thief who steals poets. To my mind this in no way diminishes the poet's insight into the emotional world of women. One may be a conduit between one's people and the gods, but it is also necessary to make a living. (I am not sure how to account for O'Hussey's explicitness in handling this convention. It may not be too far-fetched to compare the homosexual sonnets of Shakespeare.)

There is another even more famous poem in which, in my opinion, the goddess speaks by her poet. It is the much-translated lament of the Hag of Beare; or, perhaps more properly, the Nun of Beare. The old woman speaks words almost certainly put into her mouth by a votary of the goddess, almost certainly a man, who sees with the conquest of Christianity his occupation gone. The ageless divinity, the lover and spouse of Kings, is made mortal on contact with the new religion; as Oisin is in the Fenian cycle or the Children of Lir in the Tuatha Dé Danaan tales. She is widowed, old, unlovely, and sees before her only dreary conversion, virtue and death. She experiences this not only allegorically but in the actual person of her priest. Here are some of the verses the he/she figure speaks; they are taken from the masterly anthology, *A Golden Treasury of Irish Poetry* (London, 1967), compiled, with translations, by David Greene and Frank O'Connor – both, alas, now dead:

(1)

Ebb to me, unlike the sea's; old age makes me bleed. Though I may grieve at it, happily does its tide return.

(2)

I am the Nun of Bearra Baoi. I used to wear a shift that was always new. Today I have become so thin that I would not wear out even an old shift.

(3)

It is riches you love, not people; when we were alive, it was people we loved . . . .

(4)

Swift chariots and horses that won the prize, once I had plenty of them – God rest the King who gave them . . . .

(5)

Bony and thin are my hands; dear was the trade they practised, they would be around splendid kings.

(6)

Bony and thin are my hands; I swear they are not worth raising above pretty boys.

(7)

The girls are joyous when May approaches. Sorrow is more fitting for me; I am not only sad, but an old woman.

(8)

I pour out no good sweet ale, no wethers are killed for my wedding; my hair is grey and scanty, it is no loss to have a miserable veil over it.

(9)

I do not care if there is a white veil on my head; I had coverings of every colour on my head when I drank good ale . . . .

(10)

The wave of the great sea is noisy, winter has stirred it up; I do not expect nobleman or slave's son to visit me today.

(11)

It is many a day since I sailed on the sea of youth; many years of my beauty have departed because wantonness has spent itself.

(12)

It is many a day since I have been warm; I have to take my shawl even in sunlight, for old age sets on one like me.

(13)

Youth's summer that I knew I have spent with its autumn, wintry age that smothers everyone has begun to approach me.

(14)

I wasted my youth to begin with, and I am glad I decided it thus; even if I had not been venturesome, the cloak would now be new no longer . . . .

(15)

God help me! I am a poor wretch; each bright eye has decayed. After feasting by bright candles, I am in the darkness of a wooden church.

(16)

I have had my time with kings, drinking mead and wine; today I drink whey and water among withered old women . . . .

(17)

I see on myself the shaggy cloak of age – no, I am wrong: grey is the hair that grows through my skin, like the lichen on an old tree.

(18)

My right eye has been taken away, alienated for my forfeited estate, and the left eye has been taken to complete its bankruptcy.

(19)

The flood wave, and the swift ebb; what the flood brings to you the ebb carries out of your hand.

(20)

The flood wave, and the following ebb; both have come to me, so that I am well acquainted with them . . . .

(21)

Happy is the island of the great sea, for the flood comes to it after the ebb; as for me I expect no flood after ebb to come to me.

(22)

My dwelling is miserable today, so that I should recognise this: what was flooding is now all ebbing.

Closely related to this theme are the poems ascribed to Gormfhlaith, widow of three Kings: Cormac, King-Bishop of Cashel, Carroll of Leinster and Niall Glúndubh (or 'Black-Knee'). Gormfhlaith's name is the key to their significance. I like to translate it 'cerulean sovereignty'. She is Ireland lamenting three great provincial Kings, each of whom aspired to paramountcy over his fellows and each of whom paid for the attempt with his life.

A similar pattern will fit another great Gaelic romance, the love of the nun Líadan for the ex-poet Cuirithir. It belongs to the Old Irish period. In the fashion of the time, the narration was in prose and the dialogue in verse. Only notes for the narrative survive but at least some of the verse has been written out in full. Again we take Líadan as a goddess – this time specifically a goddess of poetry – who, like St. Bridget of Kildare, once the goddess of fire and the arts, has bowed to the new faith and accepted the Christian veil. When Cuirithir the poet comes to claim his bride, she is to wed the King of Heaven. Cuirithir in turn is converted and becomes a cleric bound by vows of chastity. They may never wed, but their passion endures and speaks in two lyrics attributed to Líadan. I see the story as the reflection of a difficult passage for poetry in the coming to terms with the new dispensation. Ultimately a *modus vivendi* was arrived at which distinguished roughly between secular and moral dominion and left the former to the poet; although, of course, matters could never be quite so cut and dried as that, and the church continued to encroach whenever possible on the terrain of pagan custom.

It may be worth expanding a little here on the question of namesakes and nomenclature generally, since the reference to Bridget has brought it up. The Goddess had many names – Eire, Banba, Fodhla, Bridget, Macha, Emer, Maeve. (I had a splendid professor of Old Irish when I went to the University who used to apostrophise his women students, 'I can't see what you want calling yourselves after Maeve and Emer for – Emer means granite, and Maeve means drunkenness'.) But of course people *did* call their daughters after them, and a name can stand at one and the same time for the goddess who endures and for successive heiresses and priestesses – a fruitful source of confusion. So when we read that the Abbess of Kildare, the successor of St. Bridget, was raped by Dermot Mac Murrough, the Quisling of Irish historiography, it may only meant that Dermot took the sovereignty of Leinster by force;

or, at the very worst, that he felt that in sleeping with the successor of the goddess – nun and all as she might be – he was ensuring his tenure of the sovereignty.

From classical Modern Irish and Old Irish we go forward to the eighteenth century: the Age of Reason is established in Europe, but for the beaten remnants of the Gaelic nation nothing remains except hopeless fantasies of past glories and equally hopeless fantasies of deliverance from across the sea. Here again, in the midst of all this desolation, we find the goddess installed under her various names: Eire, Banba, Fodhla and the rest. She has been brutally misused by her present rulers and pines hopelessly for her rightful Kings – sometimes for the exiled Stuarts, sometimes for some local chiefly family. This is the stuff of the Aisling, or vision-poetry as it is called, in which the poet meets, in a vision, a sky-woman of great beauty who reveals herself as Ireland, the bride of many Kings. It is a special taste. At best it has an elegiac dignity and tenderness which I think I can best convey by quoting the lyric of one of Thomas Moore's Irish Melodies. Thomas Moore is a much undervalued poet, and here his English seems to me to catch the authentic tone of the best productions of this particular genre. It cannot be overemphasized, however, that even the run-of-the-mill examples of the Aisling show extraordinary felicity of language and great metrical skill. When it is remembered that they are for the most part the work of hedge-schoolmasters and farm-labourers, they represent an extraordinary phenomenon. Like Moore's Melodies themselves, they are intended to be sung, and the wedding of the words to the music is masterly. It is consequently not easy to realise their full quality if you do not hear them sung. An excellent anthology of poems from this period – with translations – has been published in Dublin recently: *Poems of the Dispossessed*, by Seán O Tuama and Thomas Kinsella.

The influence of this vision-poetry on the Anglo-Irish literary movement has been profound: one only has to remember Yeats's Cathleen Ni Houlihan to realize that, for good or ill, the goddess is still with us in one atavar or another. Here, in one of her gentler guises, she is apprehended by Tom Moore:

The Irish Peasant to his Mistress

Through grief and through danger thy smile hath cheered my way,
Till hope seemed to bud from each thorn that round me lay;
The darker our fortune the brighter our pure love burned,
Till shame into glory, till fear into zeal was turned;
Yet, slave as I was, in thy arms my spirit felt free,
And blessed even the sorrows that made me more dear to thee.

Thy rival was honoured, while thou wert wronged and scorned,
Thy crown was of briers, while gold her brows adorned;
She wooed me to temples, whilst thou lay'st hid in caves,
Her friends were all masters while thine, alas! were slaves;
Yet cold in the earth at thy feet I would rather be,
Than wed where I loved not, or turn even in thought from thee.

Moore reportedly knew very little, if any, Irish, but he would not
have needed it to catch the mood of his distressed fellow-
countrymen; his genius could absorb it, as it were, by osmosis. It is
also true that his sky-woman here is not, technically, Ireland, but
rather the Roman Catholic Church. This is in itself significant.
Historically it was to become increasingly difficult to distinguish
between Church and Nation in the folk mind. The wheel had come
full circle, and the two personifications, erstwhile mistrustful of
each other, could be reconciled as one. Indeed so successful was the
identification of one with the other that in the years before 1916
Eoin Mac Neill, Celtic Scholar and Commander-in-Chief of the
Volunteers, also a devout Catholic, had to organise a special course
of lectures to impress on the rank-and-file that Eire, or mother
Ireland, or Cathleen Ni Houlihan, or whatever, was a pagan deity
and that the devotion lavished on her was idolatry. He could have
spared himself the trouble; in whatever avatar, she was with us yet.
Not only did she have her poets; she had her blood-sacrifice as well.
She has been demanding more of the same ever since.

At this point I should like, rather belatedly, to define my terms as
set out in the title of this piece, and perhaps to summarise what it is I
have hoped to show. I have long sensed that there was a dynamic
element, specifically felt as feminine, at work in the generating of
Irish literature, of Irish poetry in particular; that this element was
the worship of the goddess-figure and worked actively towards the
evolution of conscious poetry from ritual and liturgy – rather as
Classical Greek Drama evolved from religious ceremony. In having
to think himself into a female role – as the Greek actor did – the poet
could broaden the scope of his imaginative powers and speak with
the voice of humanity as a whole. There is no doubt in my mind that
the verse-dialogue of the sagas and the dramatic apologues of the
bardic schools were the first steps towards a Gaelic theatre, which in
more propitious circumstances might have evolved and flourished.
That its growth should have been aborted is sad, but there is perhaps
a compensating factor in that its arrested development may help us
to understand the growth of drama in other cultures. (After all, the
basic *dramatis personae* for most of us are two in number, a man and
a woman.) Here we see the notion of woman as an independent

entity forcing itself on the attention of man and, as it were, taking on his voice to express itself, so that in one human personality the dichotomy between the sexes is made whole, and the male and female principles are subsumed into a common creation.

NOTE

1   Thomas Smyth, *Information from Ireland* (1651), in *Seven Centuries of Irish Learning*, ed. Brian Ó Cuív (Dublin, 1961).

WOMEN IN THE PLAYS OF W.B. YEATS

ANDREW PARKIN

In this paper I trace the women in Yeats's plays, starting with peasant characters, moving them by way of a brief transition about loftier wives and mistresses to a consideration of the women in *The Words Upon the Window-Pane*; this is followed by discussion of noble women whose fates involve betrayal and heroism; after this two types of 'women in love' can be discerned. This leads to a discussion of magical queens or priestesses. These categories are not, of course, the only ones possible; indeed, they might be totally unsuitable for a different approach. But I have preferred the path I shall take here, because I am interested in specifically literary insight in this paper, rather than any particular ideology. Furthermore, I hope that Yeats's tendency to humanize history and legend will show up plainly, as well as a contrary tendency to dig behind the myths to seek in his characters representations of what Jung would call 'certain basic trends in the psychic process',[1] those 'categories of the imagination' which are the images or 'patterns of instinctual behaviour'.[2]

Almost of all Yeats's plays are set in the past, usually the very distant or indeterminate past. One reason a writer might do this would be that he wished to disguise his material, cover up relationships with the all-too-living, avoid embarrassments or, perhaps, lawsuits. Yeats's motives were different. He wanted settings remote in time because they could convincingly accommodate the language and conventions of poetry. He wrote about people supposedly long since dead: wives, mothers, virgins, noblewomen, mediums and queens, because he wanted to explore the literary possibilities of myth and folklore, encountering those types of the female who have lived and died and been buried many times.

It is in the early plays, written before and just after the turn of the century (sometimes with the help of Lady Gregory), that we find his portraits of peasant women, influenced no doubt by knowledge of the country people of Sligo and Gort, people for whom folklore was still alive. He had summed up the harsh lives of some of their women in his little poem, 'The Song of the Old Mother'; Yeats's persona in that poem can be found again in such dramatis personae as Bridget Bruin of *The Land of Heart's Desire*, a toiling peasant mother-in-law, a shrewish woman whose burden of household work fills her thoughts. She is an ally of the priest, of course, and can scold her husband with 'You are the fool of every pretty face'.[3] Bridget's peasant hospitality and recognition of the faery child as highly born aid in bringing the child into the house, leading of course to the very blasphemy and sacrilege Bridget is quick to recognize and which she dreads so much. Her life is condensed into the dialogue she has with the faery, who sees into Bridget's heart: the scene is a direct analogue to its other version, 'The Song of the Old Mother', and stands as a foil to offset the beguiling delicacy of the faery's song, 'The lonely of heart is withered away' (*C.Pl.*, 63). Bridget herself is a character foil, too, for the rebellious Mary, the restless new bride, the woman who rejects the conventional mould of housewife. Mary is not, however, only an Ibsen 'new woman' of the stamp of Nora; she has a puzzling disturbance of the soul, responding to mysterious forces inside and beyond her, as does the lady from the sea. Shawn recognizes that she is not merely domestic; she seeks 'light and freedom, (*C.Pl.*, 62). She flees love, church, and the safe domesticity of Bridget not for a career in the middle-class world but to seek strange lore in the book, three generations old, compiled by her father-in-law's grandfather; she dies to the life of her family, becoming one who is 'away'[4] in the other kingdom. She would destroy the world to rebuild it. She is the peasant counterpart of those masterful woman of the nobility who stalk through Yeats's dramatic world.

The Bridget type of peasant housewife appears again as Bridget Gillane, the careful, frugal, practical household organizer in *Cathleen ni Houlihan*. Vexed that she has had to work so hard to get so little, disgruntled because she started with so meagre a dowry, she is yet proud of her son, and we are left in no doubt that her son's fiancée, Delia, is getting a very good man with whom she had best be well satisfied. A tough schemer who is alert to the main task of furthering the family fortunes, Bridget also displays the counterbalances to peasant canniness: hospitality, compassion and superstitious credulity. And it is particularly important that she should bring out the possibilities of gentle compassion in the role when she comforts the pretty and artless young Delia Cahel at the end of the play. Without this, the famous curtain-line would lose much of its energy. The homely sturdiness of the peasants needs to be there, too, in order to enliven the build-up to the supernatural crises of both *The Land of Heart's Desire* and *Cathleen ni Houlihan*; peasant life also provides the sense of hard-won human order, which is suddenly seen as not so much harsh put puny, in the face of instinctual forces like the faery child or the hag of Ireland.

Yeats's third Bridget, the Wise Man's wife in *The Hour Glass*, is a woman who used to pray but has been corrupted by her freethinking husband, and is, in any case, too tired of an evening because of household chores. Yeats relishes the irony and humour of the situation, which is the undertow of his sceptic's frantic search for faith: this Bridget has been freed by her husband from one kind of superstition, but she is not by any means a freethinker or an individual in her own right. She does not dominate her man in the way of the other Bridgets. Staunchly sexist, she tells us 'O, a good wife only believes in what her husband tells her' (*C.Pl.*, 317).

If in *The Unicorn From the Stars* and *The Pot of Broth* Yeats was able to draw upon Lady Gregory's knowledge of the folk and their beliefs, her acute observation and her richly comic gifts for such characters as Biddy Lally and Sibby Coneely, it is also worth mentioning his debt to Biddy, for instance, when he comes later to create Crazy Jane. Biddy is more than a touch of local colour. She is a thieving beggarwoman, 'one of the knowledgeable women' (*C.Pl.*, 357), who sees visions at Martin's bidding and divines by means of cups of gold and silver; although she says she has abandoned prophecy on account of the 'stiffness and the swelling it brought upon my joints' (*C.Pl.*, 357), she is one of Yeats's medumistic women and, like Crazy Jane, she is not averse to a bit of fun at the expense of the clergy, as when she roundly declares 'There is no priest is any good at all but a spoiled priest' (*C.Pl.*, 372). But Yeats's most effective structural use of the peasant woman in his early plays is to my mind found in Mary Rua, the worried, practical cottager of *The Countess Cathleen*. The trait of peasant hospitality is there, together with the hard work – her stage business in the opening scene is to grind the quern – but she is more religious than superstitious. She ignores the marvels and horrors recounted by Teigue, drawing strength in the face of famine from her simple religious faith. Too proud to want her husband to beg, she remains compassionate and even asks for God's pity on the rich. Her stoicism in adversity goes together with a rural sense of courtesy, ceremony and traditions of feudal service, as when she tells the Countess Cathleen

> But first sit down and rest yourself awhile,
> For my old fathers served your fathers, lady,
> Longer than books can tell – and it were strange
> If you and yours should not be welcome here.
>   (*C.Pl.*, 7).

Mary Rua's quiet wisdom, simple logic and magnanimous nature fortify her against the devils in the play. She has a sharp nose for sniffing out devils, and, of course, promptly refuses to cook for them. She is courageous enough to curse them. The portrait is superior to the Mary of the earlier version of the play printed in the variorum edition,[5] for Yeats rapidly establishes her at the beginning as a stronger person than either Teigue or Shemus; she is independent and strong-minded, and takes blows from her husband in quarrels on account of it. The role demands that a mature, efficient woman be projected, one capable of eating the nettle, dock and dandelion, and of ultimately dying rather than selling out to foreign (i.e. British) materialism. Morally, she dominates her household and, structurally, provides the peasant heroism which is the sub-plot to the story of Cathleen's own destiny. Dramatically, she subtly contrasts with Cathleen's nurse, and foster-mother, Oona, whose practicality includes the philistinism of her response to Aleel's exquisite but doom-laden song:

> But the dance changes,
> Lift up the gown,
> All that sorrow
> Is trodden down.
> *(C.Pl.,* 19).

When the song is over, Oona gives him short shrift, calling him 'The empty rattle-pate!' *(C.Pl.,* 19). Oona, unlike Mary, is the kind of Christian who fears experience and lacks charity. She and Aleel, foils to each other, enrich the setting in which the heroine[6] and her counterpart, Mary Rua, make their choices against sexual love and domestic life, and in which plot and sub-plot move rapidly towards death. Mary's death provides a preliminary climax, structurally foreshadowing the death of Cathleen herself.

After the early plays, Yeats's dramatic world contains schemers of a different sort. Instead of women striving to keep a peasant home together, we find wives vying for supremacy in the pecking order in *The Green Helmet*; wives and mistresses struggling for the man in *The Player Queen*, and in *The Only Jealousy of Emer*, where they become allies against the wiles of Fand, their supernatural rival. In *The Words upon the Window-Pane* ghosts relive their bitter triangle; and, ultimately, in *The Death of Cuchulain*, wife and mistress play out their destinies under the baleful power of the Morrigu, the crow-headed war-goddess.

The Words Upon the Window-Pane, the only play of Yeats's maturity to use the conventions of realism in the theatre, is an interesting variant because it consciously links the past to contemporary life, as do *Purgatory* and *The Death of Cuchulain*. Set in the present, it is the only play of Yeats to portray contemporary urban middle-class characters. Mrs. Mallet and Miss MacKenna are contemporary women symmetrically balanced against the ghosts of Stella and Vanessa. The contrast between the passionate eighteenth-century ghosts and the modern women who are small-town busybodies obviously helps to make more vivid the Swiftian view in the play and the satire of contemporary life. But this should not blind us to certain links between the characters. Mrs. Mallet, a 'very experienced spiritualist' (*C.Pl.*, 600), a bit bossy, protective of Mrs. Henderson the medium, and solicitous for her comfort, is direct, forceful, a bit of a manager, and willing to venture to Folkestone and set up a tea-shop there. This accords with Vanessa's willingness to follow Swift from London to Dublin and there probe Stella, tackling her directly on the question of Stella and Swift's possible marriage. Although Vanessa is hurt when she thinks that her mind was shaped by Swift not out of love but as a kind of art, 'a painter's canvas' (*C.Pl.*, 609), this mind, formed by masculine ideas, links with Mrs. Mallet's dependence upon her husband's advice: 'He advises me about everything I do,' she declares, ' and I am utterly lost if I cannot question him' (*C.Pl.*, 603). Her husband has been dead for ten years. He is her oracle. Miss MacKenna, 'our energetic secretary' (*C.Pl.*, 597), an organizer, a lodger in this haunted house where Mrs. Henderson, the medium, also lives, has attended many seances, sometimes sceptical of them and sometimes impressed; she is excited enough to draw Corbett's attention to the first mention of Stella by Mrs. Henderson, speaking as the ghost of Swift; and her liking for a flutter on the dogs at Harold's Cross finds its analogue in Stella's 'certain small sums of money she has lost at cards' (*C.Pl.*, 599). These connections between the living and the dead women serve to make us prefer the sensuality, the tenderness and the desire of Vanessa, and to long, too, for Stella's complementary qualities of intelligence, poetic sensibility, and the moral realism admired by Swift when his ghost speaks to her:

With what scorn you speak of the common lot of women 'with no endowments but a face–'
> 'Before the thirtieth year of life
> A maid forlorn or hated wife.'
>
> (*C.Pl.*, 612)

Stella and Vanessa are powerful, complementary females but, although both sacrifice themselves on the altar of Jonathan Swift – and for this his spirit must purge itself by means of turbulent dreaming-back through the intensities of his life – it is Vanessa's ghost which speaks, not Stella's. Vanessa, too, is perhaps suffering still, like Swift. Stella, with her particular brand of moral heroism, has already passed to some other stage of soul-toil.

For all his concern with spirituality, the mature Yeats is earthy enough to know that higher things grow from things that are of the earth, earthy. The intricacies of thought, passion and suffering in the mind of Swift emanate from the homely, usually courteous lips of the frugal Dubliner, Mrs. Henderson, described by Dr. Trench as 'A poor woman with the soul of an apostle' (*C.Pl.*, 598). Yeats also makes clear Dr. Trench's knowledge of Swift and the history of the house; it is equally clear that Mrs. Henderson's startling dramatization of Swift's suffering could be feeding on the thoughts and desires of plodding Dr. Trench and the eager, somewhat earnest Mr. Corbet. But whether old Mrs. Henderson has been dramatizing thoughts emanating from two modern middle-class males or from a great genius long since dead, who now possesses her, we can hardly fail to recognize the miraculous beauty which sweeps aside the petty bourgeois concerns of those who attend her seance. They are annoyed, little Lulu is frightened and Mrs. Henderson exhausted by the power and the knowledge of Swift. Stella and Vanessa strike us as women of beauty, courage and strength; they are noble individuals, yet types of ideal intellectual and physical beauty, largely fashioned by their man. We apprehend them, in fact, as products of the male mind of Swift. By a Yeatsian irony, though, that male mind finds its expression through the unlettered female mind of Mrs. Henderson.

Swift's refusal to marry Vanessa for fear of passing on pollution and disease leads to the purgatorial suffering of Swift himself and possibly of Vanessa. Yeats's last treatment of this theme occurs of course in the almost unbearable tragedy, *Purgatory*. The Old Man in that play is gripped by a Swiftian hatred of common humanity, which includes his own father and son. The implacable purpose which leads to catastrophe he seems to have inherited from his grandmother. On learning that her daughter was marrying a groom, she had never spoken to her again. The chain of suffering the Old Man seeks to end began with the grandmother's horror of marriage outside her class. But the Old Man's mother, a ghost dreaming back over her desecration by her groom, never expresses any of the horror the Old Man feels. It is the Old Man's interpretation which feeds on class-hatred. From an earlier Yeatsian viewpoint, the mother and her groom might appear as modern actors in the ritual of Queen and Swineherd that we find in *A Full Moon in March*, where the incarnation of spirit is presented as a ritual of 'desecration and the lover's night' (*C.Pl.*, 629). Indeed, in *Purgatory* the marriage of lady and groom is described in extraordinary and ambiguous terms:

> She had a horse at the Curragh, and there met
> My father, a groom in a training stable,
> Looked at him and married him.
>
> (*C.Pl.*, 683)

She buys a breeding man as she might a horse. It is an action imperious, matriarchal, but a betrayal of her class. That is what her mother cannot forgive; and that is what is so hateful to her son that he goes mad trying to stem the consequences of her action. The suffering of the Old Man with his fantasy of the wedding night and the throbbing of phallic hoofbeats is never in doubt; the suffering of his mother, however, is always in doubt. It may be that she enjoys the re-enactment of her wedding-night. It may be, when she 'Looked at him and married him', she led her groom, or was led by him, into an ancient ritual both were born to enact, an instinctive phallism beyond reason and conscience. This lady's 'love at first sight' is profoundly ambivalent. A young lady loses her head, marries beneath her for love, dies in childbirth and leaves behind her a crazy, bloody chain of squalor; or a young lady is taken by a phallic horse god in the shape of a groom to unleash murder and class hatred on the land. The father is not merely a man; he is 'A dead, living, murdered man' as 'He leans there like some tired beast' (*C.Pl.*, 687). Half-drunk. Such are the instruments of the gods. *Purgatory* is Yeats's last and most brutal treatment of theophany. From this point of view, the struggle to prevent a mother's ghost from suffering is really a crazy struggle against Priapus by means of symbolic castration. By killing his father, the Old Man has castrated him. By killing his son, he has castrated both the boy and, symbolically, himself.

The Mother in *Purgatory* is akin to Dervorgilla's ghost in *The Dreaming of the Bones* in that both are noblewomen whose sexual appetites lead them into crimes of a national significance, the contemporary class-warfare and the historical Norman invasion. Although Dervorgilla is not forgiven by the young gunman, there is a good deal of sympathy for her, as there is for the Mother in *Purgatory*. Whatever their crimes in the eyes of the living, this much may be said for them (and it is no mean claim): they loved even to the edge of doom. In these two plays Yeats showed an unearthly yet very human female eroticism, sweet and touching. This female eroticism recreates the music of a lost kingdom, but it also urges a

new mood of love and forgiveness in Yeats's Ireland, a mood
expressed by female characters and denied by the males. The
change in Ireland's status and the weariness with bloodshed and
suffering perhaps go a long way towards explaining Yeats's shift
from his earlier expression of patriotic values in the fierce female
figure of Cathleen ni Houlihan. She is the loathly lady, the fatal
woman of Nationalism, seducing young men from marriage to
pursue the eroticism of battle.[7] The later Yeats was not so scornful
of domesticity. He was married. And he had lived through warfare
and atrocities:

> a drunken soldiery
> Can leave the mother, murdered at her door,
> To crawl in her own blood, and go scot-free;
>
> We, who seven years ago
> Talked of honour and of truth,
> Shriek with pleasure if we show
> The weasel's twist, the weasel's tooth.[8]

It is to the period before the Great War that Yeats's most exten-
sive studies of heroic noblewomen belong. They are, of course,
those opposing legends of female beauty, Countess Cathleen and
Deirdre. Cathleen is beautiful and aristocratic, dignified without
self-importance, virtuous but not self-righteous, gracious yet never
condescending. By this kind of balance Yeats avoids thrusting upon
us a saint that we can do without. He makes her convincing in other
ways too: her charity is generous and even-handed but not uncon-
sidered, for she is responding directly to the suffering brought by the
famine. She needs music to calm herself because of her sensitivity to
suffering. Her faith in God goes together with her sharp sense of the
uniqueness of the human soul, qualities which mark her off from the
self-righteous Oona. When Oona complains that starving people
are looting, Cathleen explains God's forgiveness of sin in terms of
His love for the individuality of each soul:

> There is no soul
> But it's unlike all others in the world,
> Nor one but lifts a strangeness to God's love
> Till that's grown infinite, and therefore none
> Whose loss were less than irremediable
> Although it were the wickedest in the world.
> (*C.Pl.*, 21)

But her faith and innocence do not mean that she is merely naïve.

Yeats adds to the credibility of the portrait by showing her awareness of evil. In searching for her castle in the wood, she believes she may be worldly enough to have lost that fortress of good, and she has enough sense and humour to know that a crochety old nurse and a dream-tormented young lover like Aleel cannot lead her back to goodness. Furthermore, she realizes very quickly that the good cannot be insulated from the world, 'for the old worm o' the world/Can eat its way into what place if pleases' (*C.Pl.*, 7). Above all, what makes her virtue credible is the conflict she feels before making the sacrifice of her soul. She knows that she must give up the love of Aleel for the sake of her people, and she cannot do it without a struggle:

> Would my imagination and my heart
> Were as little shaken as this holy flame!
> (*C.Pl.*, 28)

She feels a very natural foreboding as the certainty grows in her that she must give up her soul to the underworld:

> But I have come to a strange thought. I have heard
> A sound of wailing in unnumbered hovels,
> And I must go down, down –
> (*C.Pl.*, 34)

Like Persephone she will go down amid the death of crops; like Eurydice she is bitten by the serpent (the devil of Christian myth), and her lover is a poet, and he must not look back at her. Yeats uses the *tabu* of the Orpheus myth to intensify Cathleen's love sacrifice and the moment of parting; his poetry brilliantly blends the Irish and Greek mythology:

> There have been women that bid men to rob
> Crowns from the Country-under-Wave or apples
> Upon a dragon-guarded hill, and all
> That they might sift the hearts and wills of men,
> And trembled as they bid it, as I tremble
> That lay a hard task on you, that you go,
> And silently, and do not turn your head.
> Good-bye; but do not turn your head and look:
> Above all else, I would not have you look.
> (*C.Pl.*, 28)

But for all that, she is, touchingly, simply a woman whose lover has just left:

I never spoke to him of his wounded hand,
And now he is gone.

(*C.Pl.*, 28)

Cathleen is a role that demands an actress with simple dignity, great beauty and the emotional range to dominate the other characters, particularly the merchants. Her death-bed speech makes its quiet farewells in contrast to the high passion of Aleel and the cosmic battle that follow her death. She must therefore convey the power and stature, the greatness of soul, in Cathleen which will make the high tension of the ending seem fitting rather than overpowering.

Cathleen is Yeats's highest type of Christian woman; Deirdre is all pagan. In Yeats's version of the legend she is of unknown origin, 'a child with an old witch to nurse her,/And nobody to say if she were human,/Or of the gods' (*C.Pl.*, 172). Her beauty, like Helen's, is so great that it must bring trouble. In the exposition of the play the First Musician gives us a clear impression of Deirdre's boldness – it may be that *she* wooed Naoise before he carried her off beyond the reach of Conchubar. Yeats makes Deirdre the strongest character in the play, for she can even outscheme Conchubar. Yet Deirdre and Naoise are destroyed. The reason is that Naoise and Fergus uphold a male code of chivalric honour, a *comitatus*, which can only discount Deirdre's better judgment, a judgment shared by the other women in the play, the Musicians. The women know the power of human passions, especially an old king's jealousy. Both Naoise and Fergus, stupidly obstinate in clinging to their male code of honour, insult Deirdre and her intelligence. As she gets worried, Naoise tells her 'We must not speak or think as women do' (*C.Pl.*, 180); and that means turn to superstition and omens. A stroke of irony follows, for Yeats has Naoise unable to see far into the wood 'Because we are blinded by the leaves and twigs' (*C.Pl.*, 181). Unable to see the wood for the trees, he is irritated and ashamed by Deirdre's scheme for escape. 'Crazy fantasy' and 'gossip of the roads' (*C.Pl.*, 181) is how old Fergus dismisses the Musicians' accurate diagnosis of Conchubar's morbid sexuality and its possible outcome. In this play males are dupes; even Conchubar does not outwit Deirdre. The clash of female and male here does not follow the simplistic stereotype of intuition versus reason. Deirdre and the Musicians are realists, their realism based upon their understanding of human feeling. The wiles of Deirdre are founded (in *both* her persuasion scenes) upon her knowledge of male attitudes. In the earlier scene when she attempts to persuade Naoise to flee and save their lives, she plays on male possessive jealousy, pretending to wear her jewels for Conchubar's sake, and even uses the stereotype of the fickle woman which, in a bitterly ironic moment, Naoise hurls back at her:

> What woman is there that a man can trust
> But at the moment when he kisses her
> At the first midnight?
>
> (*C.Pl.*, 185)

Needless to say, Deirdre's motive for using her intelligence, deception or artfulness against Naoise's stubborn conventional code is to save his life. Her sheer physical courage and wild extravagance blend with steely calculation as she resolves to mar her own beauty to make Conchubar lose interest in her. When Naoise is eventually forced to see that Conchubar has no intention of keeping faith, he is given some windy rhetoric by Yeats, but he never apologizes to Deirdre, admitting error, nor tries to comfort her. By contrast, Deirdre, realist that she is, adult that she is, turns to Fergus to forgive him, and displays a cool aphoristic wit:

> You thought the best, and the worst came of it;
> We listened to the counsel of the wise,
> And so turned fools.
>
> (*C.Pl.*, 188)

Deirdre is not predictable in the way the male characters are. She sits down to await capture, but cannot go through the empty chess game to imitate previous doomed lovers. But she is concerned about reputation, in the sense of leaving fit matter for the long-remembering harpers and their songs. This is why she takes the knife from the Musician and gives her a bracelet to ensure she will sing the true story of Deirdre's ending.

The last part of the play reveals the great nobleness of Deirdre, willing to sacrifice herself for Naoise's freedom, and, in the second and this time successful persuasion scene, reveals, too, all the wiliness and bold psychological warfare of which she is capable. After direct pleading has failed, she flatters Conchubar, pretending that he knows the inner thoughts of women:

> Although we are so delicately made,
> There's something brutal in us, and we are won
> By those who can shed blood. It was some woman
> That taught you how to woo.
>
> (*C.Pl.*, 199)

Deirdre uses for her own purposes a variety of common attitudes, knowing that Conchubar would like to be thought a good and subtle

lover, knowing that he would like to think he knows the minds of
women ('You know too much of women to think so') (*C.Pl.*, 199);
knowing, too, that he wants to hear that man is master and woman
subservient, that by asking a small favour he might grant it to seal
the beginning of their relationship, and that he would want to think
he will be a better lover than Naoise: 'You'll stir me to more passion
than he could' (*C.Pl.*, 200). And when these fail, Deirdre turns to
sexual insults, but, brilliantly, she uses the tone of a wife. There is
insult and intimacy combined. Mocking Conchubar's male jealousy,
she subtly assumes she is already *his* queen, thus making him feel
more secure, and making him feel more the affront to his status and
to her as his property, if the black soldiers are permitted to humiliate her by a search. It is these latter appeals (to Conchubar's sense
of his own position, dignity and pride of ownership) which win the
argument of the scene. But much besides has been accomplished:
Yeats has given us his most complex portrait of a legendary figure,
in speeches crammed with sexuality and what might now be called
'sexism'. After this splendidly rich revelation of Deirdre's full
womanhood the end is swift, her purpose unswerving, and we
experience the full sense of waste and loss associated with tragedy.
But tragic exaltation is also there, achieved by the magnificent song.
Deirdre's entrance to the play and her exit from it are marked by
songs, lyrics of austere yet moving simplicity, which celebrate their
subject by denying their own effectiveness and art:

> What is all our praise to them
> That have one another's eyes?
> (*C.Pl.*, 178)

they sing when the lovers enter. And while Deirdre kills herself:

Second Musician. Though we were bidden to sing, cry nothing loud.
First Musician. They are gone, they are gone.
Second Musician.   Whispering were enough.
First Musician. Into the secret wilderness of their love.
Second Musician. A high grey cairn. What more is to be said?
First Musician. Eagles have gone into their cloudy bed.
> (*C.Pl.*, 202)

It is not only female and male sensibilities that have clashed in the
play, but the call of young romantic love against the premeditated
mating of the king:

> I, being King, did right
> In choosing her most fitting to be Queen,
> And letting no boy lover take the sway.
> (*C.Pl.*, 203)

Defiant words. But they are deceitful as Conchubar himself. Naoise *did* 'take the sway' for several years, while the king never did, not for a moment.

Deirdre is to me the most fascinating and liveliest role among Yeats's various portraits of women in love. The Player Queen is a comic version of the role, but on a smaller scale. Decima is what Deirdre might have become had she lived happily with Naoise until love had decayed. She plays out the comedy of marriage and the sexual tensions of a touring company. The Prime Minister, a Conchubar seen in a comic distorting mirror, says he knows her type – the difficult woman, 'a bladder full of dried peas for a brain, a brazen, bragging baggage', one who 'would pull the world to pieces to spite her husband or her lover' (*C.Pl.*, 404). She in fact ends by marrying him. She is intelligent, cruel, devious, spirited, ungovernable, one who in the way of goddesses will need many lovers, both men and animals. She loves her own pride, extravagant action, intensity of feeling, and 'she knows every trick of breaking a man's heart' (*C.Pl.*, 414). With the panache and courage with which she faces the mob, she proves herself ready to don the mask of Queen and so fulfils the prophecy in her song about the coupling of a harlot with a seamew through the body of a drunken sailor. She is not quite Deirdre, but she is the actress capable of playing her. She is also the sacred harlot's daughter and will appear again in the guise of Attracta, priestess of the Herne, and, later still, as the Harlot in *The Death of Cuchulain*, will sing the last song of Yeats written on his death-bed. Beside Decima, the official queen of the play is a pallid little ascetic who is unlikely to have coupled with a unicorn, save in a purely symbolic sense. Beside Decima, Nona, the mistress of Septimus, is practical and mundane, a simpler, comforting woman, subservient to the male ego. Nona is to Decima what Eithne Inguba is to Emer. The quarrel between Decima and Nona is the longest scene Yeats wrote between two women characters. It is a lively dialogue, satirical of theatrical temperament, a comic view of the Abbey players misbehaving while on tour.

These opposing types of the female lover recur in Yeats's plays. As early as *The King's Threshold*, Fedelm is young, beautiful and sensible; ready to compromise to save Seanchan, she is not committed as the poet is to vision and poetry. But when she sees he is unwilling to give in to the King, she proudly supports him in his fast to the death:

> Let me be near you.
> I will obey like any married wife.
> Let me but lie before your feet.
>   (*C.Pl.*, 139)

Eithne Inguba in *The Only Jealousy of Emer* is a similar type of woman. She is loving and beautiful, but shamefaced and guilty in the presence of Emer, Cuchulain's wife. She thinks of herself as but a passing fancy of Cuchulain, but is also naïve enough to suppose that she has won him back from the dead. She appears only once more, in *The Death of Cuchulain*. Here Eithne has a larger role than Emer in terms of staging, and this is in accord with Emer's having had to renounce Cuchulain's love at the last. Eithne's role is now complicated by the fact that she comes as a messenger from Emer yet is at the same time under the spell of the Morrigu, who presides over the action and whose ritual of death the play enacts. Eithne senses the presence of the Morrigu, though Cuchulain does not. Her quarrel with Cuchulain reveals her capacity for anger and cruelty, for love and loathing. She is made more vivid by the vengeful, gloating Aoife, a good foil to Eithne. Aoife's chill adds to the desolation of Cuchulain's ending, after the great outburst in which Eithne vows a death in which

> they hammer me with a ladle, cut me with a knife,
> Impale me upon a spit, put me to death
> By what foul way best pleases their fancy.
>
> > (*C.Pl.*, 698)

The desolation is not all Cuchulain's. Yeats with a stunning blow to Eithne has Cuchulain brush this vow aside with a nasty cynicism: 'Women have spoken so, plotting a man's death' (*C.Pl.*, 698). She does not speak to Cuchulain directly again. The rapid switch from anger to devotion, the play of love and loathing within the one woman, which Yeats gives us in Eithne's last scene, is something achieved here with great compression. Yeats had long been fascinated by this essentially Shakespearean effect:[9] he had used it for Dectora in *The Shadowy Waters*, who points out the conjunction of strength and weakness in woman. Dectora's queenly dignity demands 'satisfaction upon those/Who have slain my husband' (*C.Pl.*, 154), with great courage and toughness. But she casts aside revenge, puts away thoughts of worldly wealth, secure domesticity with her new lover, and chooses instead to follow him into the unknown.

Emer, Cuchulain's wife, appears in three plays. Again an example of the masterful queen, in *The Green Helmet*, proud, quarrelsome, sexual and loving, 'She spreads her tail like a peacock and praises none but her man' (*C.Pl.*, 225). She is the only one of the three wives in the play who is named. The other two are women who get their kudos from the husbands' rank; their sense of self-worth is merely the pride they take in their husbands' looks and high birth. Emer delights in Cuchulain's being the 'pithier' man, and her love-song demonstrates that she admires what he is; it asserts her own worth above others' as a complementary force to her man. Although the play is about the possible resolution of quarrels and war, Cuchulain appearing as the magnanimous superman who can impose peace, marriage is *not* presented as an equal partnership. Cuchulain is dismissive of Emer's heroism. She has great personal courage, her emotions are strong, and her love is simply and directly declared. She would kill herself for him. He shrugs this off with 'Bear children and sweep the house' (*C.Pl.*, 243). He tells her she is wise enough to marry someone else after he is dead. It is the same thought he has when he leaves his mistress before going to his last battle. Emer has the moral superiority, the finer feeling. 'It is you, not your fame that I love' she says, and rather than see him die she cries out 'Live and be faithless still' (*C.Pl.*, 242).

It is this finer spirit which provides Emer with her tragic moment in *The Only Jealousy of Emer*, when she defeats Fand, her rival, but also herself by renouncing Cuchulain's love for ever. The mature Emer of this play shows her wisdom and tolerance in her dealing with Eithne Inguba. She also has the courage to face the grotesque god Bricrui, and the greater courage to face Cuchulain's faithlessness. Fand the immortal is the only female who can arouse Emer's jealousy. Emer wants to knife her. Through her jealousy Emer brings Cuchulain back, though this costs her his love. She loses him; Fand loses him. Fand, though jealous of Cuchulain's mortal women, recognizes the worth of Emer and Cuchulain's lustful blindness to that worth:

> Being among the dead you love her
> That valued every slut above her
> While you still lived.
>
> (*C.Pl.*, 293)

Yeats's last vision of Emer is her dance before the severed heads in *The Death of Cuchulain*. Cuchulain's head is put atop a pedestal to make it a Celtic phallic symbol.[10] Emer dances her worship of the phallus; in the silence we hear 'a few faint bird notes' (*C.Pl.*, 704). The head has spoken, as in ancient myth, but it has changed its throat for the throat of a bird. Delving below the surface of human individuality, Yeats seeks the archetypal: Emer has taken her place as the Great Mother beside another type of female in the plays, the Ledaean Queen or magical priestess who mates with the god.

Cuchulain's mother was one of them. In *On Baile's Strand*

Cuchulain tells us: 'That clean hawk out of the air/ . . . begot this body of mine/Upon a mortal woman' (*C.Pl.*, 257). The clash of male and female sensibilities found in *Deirdre* is stated overtly in *On Baile's Strand*. Whereas men will be bound by oaths to conform to some impersonal code of honour or fealty to a lord, there are women who with Aoife's 'high, laughing, turbulent head' express like the Sidhe the 'will of woman at its wildest' (*C.Pl.*, 261). The Singing Women in the play, who know custom and lore, magical spell and ritual, know that such women, especially in immortal form, bring disaster. They have a capacity for love and hatred and total self-abandon. Their worship of the god is profoundly sexual. In *Cavalry*, even, Yeats shows the Christian version of this orgiastic worship:

> Martha, and those three Marys, and the rest
> That live but in His love are gathered round Him.
> He holds His right arm out, and on His arm
> Their lips are pressed and their tears fall; and now
> They cast them on the ground before His dirty
> Blood-bedabbled feet and clean them with their hair.
>
> (*C.Pl.*, 453)

The First Musician's song points out that under another dispensation such women would worship a different god (eagle, swan, gull or heron). In *The Resurrection*, a woman is seen copulating in the streets because 'She thinks the surrender to some man the dance threw into her arms may bring her god back to life' (*C.Pl.*, 586). Whether the god be Christ or Dionysus matters little, for this kind of cult worship has origins older than both.

The staring virgin who presides at the opening of *The Resurrection* is powerfully conjured up in the words of the song which describe her ritual slaughter of Dionysus in which she can tear out the heart 'And lay the heart upon her hand/And bear that beating heart away' (*C.Pl.*, 580). In *A Full Moon in March* and *The Herne's Egg* Yeats puts her on the stage. In both these plays the Virgin presides over the ritual slaughter of the hero. Attracta in *The Herne's Egg* goes into a trance, staring but asleep, and bears on her outstretched hand not a heart but an egg.

To deal with the earlier play first, in *A Full Moon in March* Yeats brings his knowledge of early Classical and Celtic religion to bear upon the subject of the sacred marriage[11] and human sexuality. Like the choric hymn in *Hippolytus*, 'For mad is the heart of love', and that in *Antigone*, 'And he who finds thee, raves',[12] Yeats's opening song is improvised on this ancient theme: 'Should old Pythagoras fall in love/Little may he boast thereof' (*C.Pl.*, 622). Yet the madness contains wisdom. Love may turn us into fools, yet the fool is holy. The sacred marriage in the play is between the Queen and the Swineherd, the man who represents the fertility of the phallic pig. The Queen's cruel virginity is analogous to barrenness of women and of the earth in winter, just as her desire for the sacred marriage represents the desire for fertility and the wholeness of new growth. In the first part of the play, Yeats stresses the human characteristics of the Queen. She is haughty yet curious; she wants to frighten her would-be lover and humiliate him, yet wants to be wooed; she calls his story of a woman who conceived from a drop of blood 'foul', yet it is she who links the Swineherd's severed head to the story; it is she who tells him to go, but at the same time 'drops her veil' that he may see her face. The sexual overture introduces the next love-song in the play. This too is ambivalent. It is a denial of 'mere woman's cruelty', a denial of responsibility for the beheading, but in its final stanzas it adores what is has loathed, the dripping head upon a stake, that most miraculous organ which is the severed phallus, symbol of resurrection. The priestess, the virgin, mother and sometimes the hag, accomplish a sacred marriage which is the great archetype of all fertility, and therefore surpasses the common sexuality which it celebrates:

> O what innkeeper's daughter
> Shared the Byzantine crown?
> Girls that have governed cities,
> Or burned great cities down,
> Have bedded with their fancy-man
> Whether a king or clown;
>
> Gave their bodies, emptied purses
> For praise of clown or king,
> Gave all the love that women know!
> O they had their fling,
> But never stood before a stake
> And heard the dead lips sing.
>
> (*C.Pl.*, 627)

The Queen reappears with a costume change. She is now the blood-stained priestess. No longer the Virgin she is the Great Mother who has conceived, and she addresses her bridegroom's head as if it were her son, 'Child and darling, hear my song,/Never cry I did you wrong' (*C.Pl.*, 628).[13] After the miraculous song of the head, she performs an orgiastic ritual dance in which she courts the head and then embraces it, reaching her climax as she kisses its lips.

This phallism reflects not only ancient Celtic religion but that of Classical Greek and Indian religion. Yeats's play, though, sublimates the phallism into a fable of the desire of spirit for body, much as Homer made out of ancient Greek cults the lofty and beautiful Olympians. As Yeats wrote elsewhere, 'Homer is my example and his unchristened heart'.[14]

In *The Herne's Egg* Yeats draws on the ornithophilous streak in ancient religion. Attracta is a priestess of the local deity, the Great Herne or heron. The marsh birds were sacred to the Celts and it is worth remembering as Jane Harrison pointed out that 'Theseus is made to call at Delos on his way home in order to dance the crane dance'.[15] In this most Aristophanic of his plays (there are several parallels with *The Birds*) Yeats was playful, making broad farce out of his mastery of ancient and curious learning. Another Greek element may be the comic toy donkey. There is one obvious reason for having a life-size donkey on the stage: a real one would be inappropriate because surrounded by stylization and convention. Another reason is that models of animals were used in cult rituals:

Apollodorus (III.1.4) tells us that Daedalus to please Ariadne made a wooden cow on wheels, hollowed it out inside, flayed a cow, sewed the hide about his handiwork and put Pasiphaë inside. A wooden cow, a wooden horse, both hollowed to hold human beings. Both were part of some ritual gear of a magical 'sacred marriage' or a ritual of resurrection.[16]

The donkey in Yeats's play contains a Clare highwayman. Yeats hints at a comic version of the sacred marriage when the donkeys copulate at the end of the play. Attracta's sacred marriage has all the ambiguity of the ancient rituals in which temple priestesses would copulate with men, sometimes worshippers, sometimes priests, and believe that their intercourse was a sacred marriage to the God. Attracta is no exception. Like the Great Mother she is a dominant goddess with a subordinate male attendant, half son, half lover. Corney might be he, but Congal becomes the true attendant when he keeps the tryst on the mountain and dies. She lives according to custom. She is simply the latest in a line of female incarnations stretching over 1,000 or 10,000 years, living among the rocks as brides of the Great Herne. Congal comes and conquers Tara, killing Aedh, his rival king. If Attracta has become the saint of the Herne god, Congal has become the Hunchback of Yeats's system who later meets the Fool. His desecration of the hernery, the stealing of the eggs and the sevenfold rape of Attracta are his blasphemies against the local god. To Congal the rape is a kind of cure for a pathological virginity. Male narcissism meets female narcissism and both are punished. The rape is priapic ceremony, and this is made plain by the fearsome phallic beat, with the table-leg, performed by Mike before the rape. For Attracta, the rape is her mystic marriage to the god. Her body is really inviolate, for she tells us 'I burn/Not in the flesh but in the mind' (*C.Pl.*, 650), and her mind is on the Herne. Like the great Mother's, Attracta's rites of marriage are also bound up with death and birth, and this is why she tells us 'To the unbegotten I return/All a womb and a funeral urn' (*C.Pl.*, 650). By raping her, Congal has made her womb into his own funeral urn.

The other three women in the play, the girls who bring gifts to Attracta, serve to suggest the worshippers of the local cult. They also suggest the women who worship Christ in *Calvary*. One of them is called Mary, and it is she who is meek, afraid of the fierce men, and is fascinated by the actual details of mating with a bird, is able to interpret Attracta's dance, and prophesies about her marriage to the god. Attracta tells the other girls that one will marry a blond, the other a dark-haired boy. But to Mary she says that

> Mary shall be married
> When I myself am married
> To the lad that is in her mind.
> (*C.Pl.*, 653)

The dove entered Mary's head. It is clear that Mary will be the next Virgin and Mother. The donkey conceived at the end of the play is a joke played on Congal, but it will also become the donkey that carries the next god, Christ, on Palm Sunday. And then when Calvary comes around the joke will be on the Herne, for he will be the vanquished god of a spent epoch:

> Motionless under the moon-beam,
> Up to his feathers in the stream;
> Although fish leap, the white heron
> Shivers in a dumbfounded dream.
> (*C.Pl.*, 449)

In *The Herne's Egg* Yeats springs on us a self-parody, at once funny and mysteriously profane. In this, his late vision, Attracta is the victim of a brutal rape; she is also an archetype – one of an ancient line of most highly favoured ladies.

NOTES

1   C.G. Jung, 'Relations between the Ego and the Unconscious' in Joseph Campbell, ed., *The Portable Jung* (Harmondsworth: Penguin, 1978), p. 75.

2   C.G. Jung, 'The Concept of the Collective Unconscious' in Campbell, *The Portable Jung*, pp. 60, 61.

3   W.B. Yeats, *Collected Plays* (London: Macmillan, 1953), p. 59. Further references to this edition will be cited parenthetically as *C.Pl.*, giving page number only.

4   To investigate this notion further see Lady Augusta Gregory, *Visions and Beliefs in the West of Ireland Collected and Arranged by Lady Gregory: With Two Essays and Notes by W.B. Yeats* (1920; Gerrards Cross: Colin Smythe, New York: Oxford, 1970), pp. 104–147.

5   See *The Countess Kathleen* in Russell K. Alspach, ed., *The Variorum Edition of the Plays of W.B. Yeats* (London: Macmillan, 1966), pp. 2–168. In this earlier version, Mary Rua is far more superstitious. She is shrewish rather than sturdily independent, hysterical in her resistance to the devils, and is denied the bitter scene Yeats devises for the later Mary Rua, who lies dead while her husband curries favour with the devils by calling her a fool. In the early version, we simply learn she is dead from the Second Merchant. (For thorough discussion of revisions in Yeats's plays see Bushrui, *Yeats's Verse Plays: The Revisions 1900–1910* [Oxford, New York: Clarendon, 1965].)

6   It is worth noting Yeats's use of the Shakespearean trio of heroine, nurse and lover for the dramatization of spiritual rather than sexual choice.

7   The symbolic Cathleen has enough power in Irish tradition to stand alone, but her mixture of fierceness and the erotic suggests some evolution from the Sheelagh na Gig figures. Cathleen's change from hag to queen of course finds its classical parallel in the goddess Demeter who, at Eleusis, dropped her disguise as crone and strode away:

Then as she spake – the goddess cast away her stature old
And changed her shape in wondrous wise, and beauty manifold
She breathed around. From forth her robe a perfumed fragrance shed
That makes the heart to yearn. Her golden hair about her head
Streamed and her flesh celestial through the goodly chambers glowed –
Like lightning fire from forth the halls, straightaway the goddess strode.
'Hymn to Demeter' quotedin Jane Harrison, *Mythology*. (New York: Cooper Square Publishers, 1963, p. 86)

8   'Nineteen Hundred and Nineteen' in W.B. Yeats, *Collected Poems* (London: Macmillan, 1952), pp. 233 and 235–236.

9   *Richard III,* Act 1, scene 2.

10 See Anne Ross, *Pagan Celtic Britain* (London: Routledge and Kegan Paul, 1967), p. 63.

11 For further discussion of the sacred marriage see Gilbert Murray, *Four Stages of Greek Religion* (New York: Columbia Univ. Press, 1912) and Jane Harrison, *Mythology* (New York: Cooper Square Publishers, 1963).

12 See Harrison, pp. 108–110.

13 Cf. Harrison's description of 'the dominant goddess with the . . . male attendant, half-son, half-lover' in Harrison, p. 65.

14 W.B. Yeats, *Collected Poems* (London: Macmillan, 1952), p. 286.

15 Harrison, p. 54.

16 Harrison, pp. 45–46.

SYNGE AND THE NATURE OF WOMAN

ANN SADDLEMYER

Maurya of *Riders to the Sea*, Pegeen Mike of *The Playboy of the Western World*, Deirdre of the Sorrows, all are acknowledged leading figures in the hierarchy of twentieth-century drama. What has less often been observed (although more so recently)[1] is that in nearly all of Synge's plays the women are not only more clearly defined than most of the men but also treated with a sympathetic complexity which frequently determines plot, mood and theme. Even the jaunting, joy-ridden Christy Mahon is delineated and nourished by the two women who battle for possession, Pegeen and the Widow Quin. That very parricide which catapults him into mythic glory is initiated by his father's wily attempts to mate him with the fearsome Widow Casey – half-horror, half-nurse, surely in herself a veiled parody of the hag-goddess of sovereignty, the 'loathly lady', with a touch of insatiable Medbh thrown in for good measure:

A walking terror from beyond the hills, and she two score and five years, and two hundredweights and five pounds in the weighing scales, with a limping leg on her, and a blinded eye, and she a woman of noted misbehaviour with the old and young . . . He was letting on I was wanting a protector from the harshness of the world, and he without a thought the whole while but now he'd have her hut to live in and her gold to drink . . . 'I won't wed her,' says I, 'when all know she did suckle me for six weeks when I came into the world, and she a hag this day with a tongue on her has the crows and seabirds scattered, the way they wouldn't cast a shadow on her garden with the dread of her curse.'[2]

As the Mayoites learn to their cost, Christy Mahon escapes this gruesome Oedipal fate (to kill a father and marry with a mother); he also escapes finally from dependency, when, thanks to one woman, he is freed from hiding behind the skirts of another.[3] There is a fittingly heroic analogue in Old Mahon, himself vividly described in the midst of delirium tremens 'shying clods again the visage of the stars', recognizing Christy the new-found Playboy, 'I'd know his way of spitting and he astride the moon'. But it is Woman who has

58

made that heroism possible through the act of recognition.

It is Pegeen who raises the broom and calls forth the beginning of a tale till then existing in the delighted curiosity of Christy's inquisitors alone, who can only reflect their private meaner, darker inclinations:

PEGEEN. He's done nothing, so. If you didn't commit murder or a bad nasty thing, or false coining, or robbery, or butchery or the like of them, there isn't anything would be worth your troubling for to run from now. You did nothing at all . . . .
CHRISTY [*offended*]. You're not speaking the truth.
PEGEEN [in mock rage]. Not speaking the truth, is it? Would you have me knock the head of you with the butt of the broom?
CHRISTY [*twisting round on her with a sharp cry of horror*]. Don't strike me . . . I killed my poor father. Tuesday was a week, for doing the like of that.

It is Pegeen too who turns round Christy's self-image:

You should have had great people in your family, I'm thinking, with the little small feet you have, and you with a kind of quality name, the like of what you'd find on the great powers and potentates of France and Spain.

And, with the Widow Quin's eager collusion, it is Pegeen who reinforces 'such poet's talking, and such bravery of heart':

Up to the day I killed my father, there wasn't a person in Ireland knew the kind I was, and I there drinking, waking, eating, sleeping, a quiet, simple poor fellow with no man giving me heed . . . . Well, . . . It's great luck and company I've won me in the end of time – two fine women fighting for the likes of me –, till I'm thinking this night wasn't I a foolish fellow not to kill my father in the years gone by.

Act II of *The Playboy* replaces the chorus of sly male inquisitors with an equally curious but far more joyous and imaginative chorus of young girls, led by Sara Tansey, 'the one yoked the ass cart and drove ten miles to set [her] eyes on the man bit the yellow lady's nostril on the northern shore'. Fired by tales from the papers of 'the way murdered men do bleed and drip', Sara is philosophical enough to hide her initial disappointment at not finding Christy at home by making off with his boots: 'There's a pair do fit me well, and I'll be keeping them for walking to the priest, when you'd be ashamed this place, going up winter and summer with nothing worth while to confess at all.' Nor, when the meek murderer does finally appear, is she as easily overwhelmed as the men in the shebeen the night before:

Is your right hand too sacred for to use at all? [*She slips round behind him*]
It's a glass he has. Well I never seen to this day, a man with a looking-glass
held to his back. Them that kills their fathers is a vain lot surely.

And, despite the foolery of her toast to 'the wonders of the western
world, the pirates, preachers, poteen-makers, with the jobbing jock-
ies, parching peelers, and the juries fill their stomachs selling judg-
ments of the English law' (in itself showing a remarkably clear
vision of the ambiguities of justice, culled no doubt from her avid
reading of newspapers), it is Sara Tansey who realistically but
fruitlessly alongside the Widow Quin tries to help Christy escape
from the paradox of justice he has created for himself in the last act.

   If Sara Tansey is the leader of the day-time chorus, goading
Christy into honing and refining his image as the giant-killer, and
Pegeen is the fiery image of romance which culminates in the superb
love-duet of Act III, transforming both sweating jockey and itching
barmaid into sweet singers of the rude pastoral, it is the Widow
Quin who serves as the arch linking the 'romantic' with the
'Rabelaisian' (Synge's own defensive terms for the balance of tension in the play). For in the creation of this witty, worldly, thirty-
year-old widow, Synge encourages us to enter a world of harmless
(though brutal) make-believe and sweet (though bitter) romance
while effectively preventing us from resting comfortably within that
golden pre-lapsarian world. The Widow is, after all, summoned out
of the dark by Father Reilly himself, and bidden serve as chaperon
and guardian to the unfolding of the entire play. Through her
sympathetic, affectionately scornful eye, we are invited to take note
not only of the making of the playboy but of our own eager contribution to that imaginative joy Synge celebrated as peculiar to the
locality and the richness of peasant nature. For she too is carved of
heroic stuff, though the deed itself is so close to home as to win but
'small glory with the boys itself'. Therein lies a further key to
Pegeen's later denunciation of the marvel of a strange man 'with his
mighty talk' of 'a gallous story' which becomes 'a dirty deed . . . a
squabble in your back-yard and the blow of a loy'. Marcus Quin, hit
with a rusty pick so that he never overed it, was also 'a great warrant
to tell stories of holy Ireland till he'd have the old women shedding
down tears about their feet'. And if Marcus Quin is both *in* mythology, lamented as a lost hero, and *outside* of it, felled in his own
backyard so that his 'murder' is rejected as accidental and therefore
commonplace, his Widow too is set apart, 'looking on the schoon-
ers, hookers, trawlers is sailing the sea', from her little houseen 'far
from all sides' above. Like Christy, yet unlike, her isolation has
created a breadth of sympathy and realistic appraisal not granted

her fellow villagers. She acts as foil to both Christy and Old Mahon in her lusty humour and materialism, and as counterbalance to Pegeen and the village girls in her experience and longings. Significantly it is the widow who tags Christy 'the walking playboy of the western world', with all the irony that complex title – hoaxer, humbug, mystifier, role-player and play-maker – implies. Through her eyes the west of Ireland dissolves and expands, by way of 'foxy skippers from France' and one-way tickets to the western states, to the wonderful world of make-believe, the mysterious west as opposed to the mystic east, the far side of the moon: 'when it's the like of you and me you'd hear the penny poets singing in an August fair'. Yet constantly she brings the audience back to the very border between fantasy and realism with which Synge flirts, reminding us of the transitory nature of what is being played out before us. No wonder she almost toppled the delicate balance of the play's structure more than once in earlier drafts, forcing Synge to tone down her powerful sympathies and zest for life. In the completed text, she must be given her own rejection scenes with Christy and be swept offstage before we can take full note of Pegeen's hurt. But in the reverberations of Pegeen's final lament, 'Oh my grief, I've lost him surely. I've lost the only playboy of the western world', we catch the earthy tones of the more experienced playgirl who remains behind in Mayo, rooted in that reality from which Christy has been liberated.

The Tinker's Wedding, begun at the same time as Synge's one-act plays, was not completed to Synge's satisfaction until after *The Playboy* had been produced. Not surprising, then, that we find Pegeen Mike's horizon-fever given its romantic obverse in the young travelling-woman Sarah Casey's longing for the stamp of conventionality – a wedding ring and the priest's blessing. Or that the Widow Quin's loneliness, ironic sympathy, and breadth of understanding emerge once again in that 'old flagrant heathen' Mary Byrne, whose natural generosity can embrace the trials of priesthood on the one hand, and the shrewd folk-knowledge of the outsider on the other. 'If it was the Holy Father from Rome was in it, she'd give him a little sup out of her mug, and say the same as she'd say to yourself.' Herself a great warrant for telling 'grand' stories 'of the great queens of Ireland with white necks on them the like of Sarah Casey, and fine arms would hit you a slap the way Sarah Casey would hit you', she also reminds us of the transience of both time and romance: 'what's a little stroke on your head beside sitting lonesome on a fine night, hearing the dogs barking, and the bats squeaking, and you saying over, it's a short while only till you die?' In this rollicking farce underscored by wistful sadness at the loss of a different kind of innocence from *The Playboy*'s, it is old Mary Byrne who draws together bold grotesque strokes, sweet songs to nature, and, in her realistic appraisal of the hardship of a Traveller's life, earthy good sense. Patting the Priest's head as he struggles helplessly gagged and trussed in old sacking, she offers advice which once again balances the Rabelaisian with the romantic:

That's a good boy you are now, your reverence, and let you not be uneasy, for we wouldn't hurt you at all. It's sick and sorry we are to tease you; but what did you want meddling with the like of us, when it's a long time we are going our own ways – father and son, and his son after him, or mother and daughter, and her own daughter again – and it's little need we ever had of going up into a church and swearing – I'm told there's swearing with it – a word no man would believe, or with drawing rings on our fingers, would be cutting our skins maybe when we'd be taking the ass from the shafts, and pulling the straps the time they'd be slippy with going around beneath the heavens in rains falling.

An early draft of his preface puts Synge's point of view plainly: 'The Tinker's Wedding is not a discussion of bad behaviour [but] is an attempt to catch some of the humour and freshness which is in all life, and which are the only food on which the mind can live healthily'. However, in a letter to Molly Allgood he admitted that perhaps he had this time gone too far: 'The play is good I think, but it looks mighty shocking in print'. Not even Yeats recommended its production at the Abbey.

Just as Mary Byrne, with a harsher view of reality, carries the union of sensual gusto with romantic sensibility beyond the characterization of the Widow Quin, projections of both women can be seen in the unsatisfied longings tinged with bitter awareness voiced by Nora Burke in Synge's shorter, earlier play of horizon-fever, *The Shadow of the Glen*. Old enough to take a husband ('What way would I live and I an old woman if I didn't marry a man with a bit of a farm, and cows on it, and sheep on the back hills?'), young enough to take a lover ('It's in a lonesome place you do have to be talking with someone, . . . and if it's a power of men I'm after knowing they were fine men, . . . for . . . it's a hard woman I am to please'), Nora has already conquered the need for materialist comfort which led her to marry Dan in the first place; she also has begun to face the emptiness of childlessness, the dangers of shadows which threaten her own insanity, and, the greatest fear of all, the passing of time. It is she who first recognizes in the comically shabby Tramp a kindred spirit, one whose imaginative sympathy and perceptiveness can help her find refuge in the very eye of the storm, the intensity of nature itself. But she also recognizes the quality of that refuge, when she interrupts with a fine ironic sense the Tramp's rhapsodies over grand evenings and wild nights:

TRAMP [*at the door*]. Come along with me now, lady of the house, and it's not my blather you'll be hearing only, but you'll be hearing the herons crying out over the black lakes, and you'll be hearing the grouse, and the owls with them, and the larks and the big thrushes when the days are warm, and it's not from the like of them you'll be hearing a talk of getting old like Peggy Cavanagh, and losing the hair off you, and the light of your eyes, but it's fine songs you'll be hearing when the sun goes up, and there'll be no old fellow wheezing the like of a sick sheep close to your ear.
NORA. I'm thinking it's myself will be wheezing that time with lying down under the Heavens when the night is cold, but you've a fine bit of talk, stranger, and it's with yourself I'll go.

Synge meant that ruthless undercutting to ride over the Tramp's poetry, but although Maire nic Shiubhlaigh played Nora with an innocent intensity that made some of the more puritanical members of the audience squirm with a discomfort they would never have felt at the popular theatres on the other side of the Liffey, he complained that Willie Fay as the Tramp 'is so strong he dominates the play – unconsciously and inevitably – and of course the woman should dominate'.[4] Even so, *The Shadow of the Glen*, Synge's first produced play, caused controversy, later to be explained by Yeats as the audience's rejection of 'the grotesque reality beside the vision'. For 'grotesque reality', read 'sensuality', as Synge himself recognized in his explanation to a friend for the adverse (sometimes as in the case of Maud Gonne, indignant) reaction:

On the French stage the sex-element of life is given without the other balancing elements; on the Irish stage the people *you* agree with want the other elements without sex. I restored the sex-element to its natural place, and the people were so surprised they saw the sex only.[5]

He determined with his next play to write 'like a monochrome painting, all in shades of the one colour'; Willie Fay countered that just meant all the characters were bad-tempered.[6] And certainly the picture in *The Well of the Saints* of two blind beggars groping their way through a grey and empty landscape, compounding complacent illusion with ironic vindictiveness, has little of the joy we now associate with Synge. When Mary and Martin Doul are granted the miracle of sight they are betrayed into an acceptance of the realities of an ugly, cold and jeering world; when they deliberately create new illusions for themselves they enter a deeper darkness still, beyond loneliness and blindness. Where in *The Shadow of the Glen* – and later in *The Playboy* – comic irony, the fool's aspiration for beauty and the dream, is nudged towards our world by the earthy sympathies of a sensitive woman, here tragic irony – the awareness that richness of life leads to dissolution and death – overwhelms. As the curtain falls on *The Well of the Saints* we are left with the painful memory of a grotesque old blind couple fumbling their way offstage towards the flooded rivers of the south, while outraged and jeering villagers (who had encouraged the Douls' first self-deception) linger to cast a few more stones before joining a wedding-party in the chapel above. This is more than the slamming of a door behind which Dan Burke invites Michael Dara to a peaceful drink or, later, Michael James's relief at seeing the back of Christy Mahon. Here, we are uncomfortably caught between feeling and reason: the Douls have chosen to reject the traditional boundaries of church and state, vision and revision, good and evil, saint and devil, blessing and curse – but we are all too aware that such lyrical heroics in this case lead to certain death. If this is the vision of the artist – rejection of the ugliness and harshness of our world in a daring embrace of the dangerous world of the imagination – there seems little health and no happiness in it.

Dark though the fabric may be, a lightening thread does run through it in the resilience of Mary Doul. Stunned and unbelieving, as Martin is, by the revelation of her own ugliness, she recovers the equilibrium of illusion sufficiently to take comfort in a future where once more she'd have 'a face would be a great wonder when it'll have soft white hair falling around it, the way when I'm an old woman there won't be the like of me surely in the seven counties of the east'. It is she too who introduces the fine tuning of reality at the threat of being cured once again: 'God help us, and what good'll our grey hairs be itself, if we have our sight, the way we'll see them falling each day, and turning dirty in the rain?' But despite this acknowledgement through Mary Doul of those two poles between which human nature continually swings, romance and farce, *The Well of the Saints* is Martin's play, and it is the yearnings of Martin Doul (himself a mighty dreamer perforce turned playboy) which lead the action to its bleak ending.

That grotesquerie born of romantic longings distorted through loneliness and a realistic appraisal of time's withering touch surfaces again in *Deirdre of the Sorrows* in the wild outbursts of mad Owen:

Queens get old Deirdre, with their white and long arms going from them, and their backs hooping. I tell you it's a poor thing to see a queen's nose reaching down to scrape her chin.

Owen's warning against the ravages of time is paralleled by the message of threatened death and treachery brought by Deirdre's old nurse, Lavarcham. Deirdre herself is freed therefore of the need to express these temporal concerns and can concentrate instead on how best to reserve her place in the 'story will be told forever'.

On facing the challenge of re-creation of a well-known myth, Synge was concerned, as he had been in his earlier plays, with the realization of a world spanning romance and reality, and once again it is through the characterization of Woman that he represents his grasp of both. Nora Burke, old Sarah Casey, Pegeen Mike and Christy Mahon, even Martin and Mary Doul, perhaps most of all the Tramp, had all expressed their romantic yearnings in imagery drawn from precisely observed details of Wicklow, Mayo and Aran; Nora and the Tramp in particular were closely attuned in their mystical, intuitive feeling for and response to Nature. In *Deirdre of the Sorrows* the natural world, while creating a sense of place, becomes a touchstone also for the unfolding of narrative, providing the parentheses within which the young lovers tackle Time and struggle for a natural unfolding of a tale that began long before they entered it.

The play opens on a night with thunder in the air and Deirdre abroad on the hillside gathering nuts and twigs for the morning's fire; she enters to find Conchubor, impatience rousing him to an abrupt finish to the child-queen's innocence. Naisi and his brothers seek shelter from the storm in the pleasures of wenching and feasting, his first lines to Lavarcham heralding the intensity of raw feeling which will sound throughout the play:

At your age you should know there are nights when a king like Conchubor would spit upon his arm ring and queens will stick their tongues out at the rising moon. We're that way this night, and it's not wine we're asking only.

Instead, Deirdre, 'grown to a queen', calls them to their destiny. The climax of decision is so swift, so sudden, that the play almost begins where all the previous ones have ended: on the threshold of a world of wonder and romance, a reality that transcends material concerns and fulfils half-concious yearnings. By immediately acknowledging their part in the saga, Deirdre and Naisi pass beyond the temporal into the permanent.

Throughout the next two acts emphasis is on the joy already grasped and on daring efforts to stop Time and its companion Death. For the sake of the narrative, hints throughout Act II remind us of the span of seven years spent in Alban: Conchubor's desolation, Lavarcham's trotting back and forth, Owen's annual visit, the sons of Usna as mighty hunters. But all actions conspire in the attempt to make Time stand still: Ainnle and Ardan argue for staying in the Edenic world of Alban; Lavarcham pleads with them to ignore Fergus' seductive call to nationalism; Owen lays down his life to forestall the loss of Deirdre's beauty; Conchubor himself lays claim to a bride more fitting to be his daughter. When Time is faced by the lovers, it is to question their ability to measure up to that ambition: a discarded draft has Naisi voice 'the dread is hidden in a joy's too wild'; and Deirdre acknowledges a more painful lone-someness than the yearning for fulfilment in earlier plays:

I've dread going or staying, Lavarcham. It's lonesome this place having happiness like ours till I'm asking each day, will this day match yesterday, and will tomorrow take a good place beside the same day in the year that's gone, and wondering all times is it a game worth playing, living on until you're dried and old, and our joy is gone forever.

Only when 'four white bodies are laid down together', when Deirdre and Naisi are removed forever from the moonlight of Alban and the woods of Cuan into the timelessness of legend, does Nature's wheel once more revolve. But even so, Lavarcham's final lines suggest how close the lovers came to stopping time forever:

Deirdre is dead, and Naisi is dead, and if the oaks and stars could die for sorrow it's a dark sky and a hard and naked earth we'd have this night in Emain.

Once fixed in narrative, how does the playwright ensure that these saga people not 'loosen [his] grip on reality'[7] as Synge feared they might? His answer was predictable yet still surprising: to let them do precisely that, moving further into intensity, concentrating on uniqueness of both romance and sensuality, and setting that singularity against the greater cosmos – Death and Time stripped of their institutional cloaks. The choice of saga material allowed Synge to avoid the clash between custom and instinct, the tug-of-war between 'ought' or 'should' and desire, that his earlier characters were caught up in; to set his play outside Christian and Victorian conventions from the onset instead of laughing them offstage as he does through the Priest in *The Tinker's Wedding* and through Shawn Keogh in *The Playboy*. Released of the need to place recog-nizable people in local indoor settings or nearby crossroads, he could build on their very strangeness: every character in *Deirdre of the Sorrows* is one of a kind; the words 'her like', 'his like', 'the like' reverberate through every page in the way the sea pounds through *Riders to the Sea*. No longer is the conflict that between natural instincts and yearnings and an external convention; here individual naked passions war for the same object – possession of Deirdre. Each character represents the range of passions of love itself: maternal protectiveness in Lavarcham; lust and sensual jealousy in Owen; fraternal loyalty and chivalric devotion in Ainnle and Ardan; love of country ('Comitatis') in Fergus; blind defiance of natural law in Conchubor; romanticism in Naisi; imperiousness in Deirdre herself. Even the saga conventions of the 'elopement tale' and supernatural elements are eliminated from or defused in the narrative: out went Deirdre's foreboding dream-visions, Cathbad's spells, Lavarcham's responsibility for introducing the luckless Naisi to Deirdre; any hint of 'the cup of sovereignty' was reduced to a mere identification of the High King's property in Act I and Deirdre's eavesdropping in Act II; while the razing of Emain Macha in Act III is foretold only as part of the final threnody.

It is in Synge's very attempt to remove the story of Deirdre and Naisi from the recognizable world while laying bare the natural passions belonging in that world that the paradox of the tale's ending exists, just as Deirdre and Naisi at the beginning face the paradox of living a legend. The folly of emotions uncontrolled by realism leads not to creation but to destruction. And so Act II ends with the Sons of Usna quarrelling for the first time, with Deirdre's shock of awareness over the body of Owen that 'death should be a poor untidy thing, though it's a queen that dies', and with her acknowledgement to Naisi, 'There's no safe place . . . on the ridge of the world'. Back in Ireland, the centre dissolves further: Deirdre herself briefly reneges and, desperately trying to save Naisi, seeks an unnatural compromise with Conchubor; Naisi is forced to choose between her love and his brothers', thus shattering for the first time his unity of nature; bitterness poisons the pact of perfection, so that the safety of the grave comes too late. Having once more attempted to push beyond our world into a dream-creation, Synge risks the same dark answer provided by *The Well of the Saints*.

But once again he finds his answer in the characterization of Woman. Deirdre must pull everything together, above the threat of dissolution into just another love-story, by emphasizing in her final great speeches both the human and the saga. She must include in her grief the memory of her quarrel with Naisi, thus embracing the bitterness of love as well as the sweetness; look past Conchubor ('an old man and a fool only') to greet the High King she has hitherto fled, Death; and overcome Time not by forcing it to stand still but by setting this night and these graves against the context of her past life in Alban and the future desolation of Emain Macha. Sorrow itself must finally be cast away as too familiar, 'an old shoe that is worn out and muddy', and replaced by the triumph of loneliness and the permanence of the symbol. In the words of Yeats, 'till grief itself has carried her beyond grief into pure contemplation'.[8]

Deirdre of the Sorrows was Synge's gift of his art to Molly Allgood: 'quite different from The Playboy, . . . quiet and stately and restrained . . . for you to act in'.[9] The folly of love (or that other romance, self-discovery) is replaced by the scope and grandeur of love. The play which began his career was equally biographical in inspiration: *Riders to the Sea*, based on his observations of life on Aran, was also in many ways a tribute to his own mother. Maurya is indeed an impressive figure – the rock within this island of rock, the surrounding sea threatening her identity as it does the very shores of Aran. One is tempted to strive after Pateresque excesses of lyricism in describing this pre-Christian Mother of Sorrows; beside her the merely human partially individuated efforts of Bartley, Cathleen and Nora fade into nodding significance. Even the querulous colouring of her early speeches ('who would listen to an old woman with one thing and she saying it over?') serves only to heighten the tragic grandeur of the conclusion. But Bartley is not only the son of all Aran mothers, of 'everyone is left living in the world'; there is much in him of the young John Synge, silently going about his business in the face of a mother grieving over his soul, lamenting that her youngest son cannot hear the true word and follow the path of righteousness. 'Isn't it a hard and cruel man won't hear a word from an old woman, and she holding him from the sea?'

If we have strayed into the autobiographical with *Riders to the Sea*, we are engulfed by it with his first completed (though last published) play, *When the Moon Has Set*. Undoubtedly based on his unsuccessful wooing of Cherrie Matheson, daughter of neighbouring Plymouth Brethren and so friendly with the family that Mrs. Synge could only approve of Cherrie's rejection despite her sympathy for her son's suffering, the play sets out to correct reality through art, with predictable results. In spite of the country cadences of Mary Costello, an old wanderer maddened by the grief of having rejected true love, the hero's uncle, in her youth (a dire warning for Cherrie!), there is only one voice in the play, Synge's own, and little sense of style. Compare the two 'natural' marriages, written less than six years apart, and we can only be struck by the extraordinary speed with which Synge learned his craft:

NAISI. Let Ainnle wed us . . . He has been with wise men and he knows their ways.
AINNLE [*joining their hands*]. By the sun and moon and the whole earth, I wed Deirdre to Naisi. [*He steps back and holds up his hands.*] May the

air bless you, and water and the wind, the sea, and all the hours of the sun and moon.   (*Deirdre of the Sorrows*)

SISTER EILEEN. I have left my veil in the room where your uncle is lying . . . I seem to be in a dream that is wider than I am. I hope God will forgive me. I cannot help it.

COLM. How many people ask to be forgiven for the most divine instant of their lives. Let us be wiser than they are. Here is the ring that was the sorrowful heirloom of my uncle. Give me your hand. I, the male power, have overcome with worship you, the soul of credulous feeling, the reader of the saints. From our harmonized discord new notes will rise. In the end we will assimilate with each other and grow senseless and old. We have incarnated God, and been a part of the world. That is enough. [*He takes her hand.*] In the name of the Summer, and the Sun, and the Whole World, I wed you as my wife. [*He puts the ring on her finger.*]

CURTAIN

(*When the Moon Has Set*)

During the summer months of 1902, while staying with his mother in Tomriland House, an old farmhouse in County Wicklow, Synge wrote *Riders to the Sea*, *In the Shadow of the Glen*, and the first drafts of *The Tinker's Wedding*. He dropped the first two plays off at Coole Park in September for Yeats and Lady Gregory to read while he paid what was to be his final visit to Aran. Within six months he was also to make a last, brief trip to Paris. The two one-act plays, which were soon to be accepted by Willie Fay's Irish Dramatic Company, make revealing companion pieces. Once having written *Riders to the Sea*, Synge was never again to tackle such atonal writing; *The Shadow of the Glen* on the other hand led him into rich, fruitful and ever more challenging explorations of the relationship between fantasy and reality, yearning and daring, romance and folly, away from the bareness of Aran into the lushness of the eastern world. It could well be that his brief encounters on Aran (and later, even more briefly, in Kerry and the Blaskets) with the 'wonderfully humorous, simple, attractive' primitive young women[10] may have been the 'shock of new material' (again his own phrase) which created style; certainly his subject-matter changed radically. But I think we must look further than those few experiences to find the key to his apparently sudden awareness of feminine nature, especially in the role he gives it in his later plays. In fact, if we examine the biographical facts more closely, eschewing the unthinking acceptance of early critical studies describing a quiet, undemonstrative, morose, reticent man, 'that slow, meditative man', whose friendships were few and whose oppressive home-life stunted any natural companionships until the seventeen-year-old flirtatious Molly swept him off his country-shod feet, we find a much more convivial, easy-mannered man, with a quiet wit and no hesitation in expressing his opinions.

Listen to the much maligned Cherrie: 'When he was interested he spoke with the greatest rapidity . . . in the evenings he used to expand and discuss Art and Poetry. . . . The next winter he went to Paris for the first time. From there he wrote me long letters telling about his life, his hardships, and experiences. Though he had hardships I don't think he minded them much; they were all more or less of an adventure. . . . Sometimes he began a word in the middle, as if he were thinking much faster than he could write. . . . He had fallen in love with [Paris], and said Ireland seemed stagnant after the life there. He said: "It is very amusing to me coming back to Ireland to find myself looked upon as a Pariah, because I don't go to church and am not orthodox, while in Paris amongst the students I am looked upon as a saint, simply because I don't do the things they do, and many come to me as a sort of Father Confessor and wish they could be like me".'[11]

John Butler Yeats: 'His conversation, like his book on the Aran Islands, had the charm of absolute sincerity, a quality rare among men and artists, though it be the one without which nothing else matters. . . . He neither deceived himself nor anybody else, and yet he had the enthusiasm of the poet.'[12]

Louis Esson, the Australian writer: 'He was a scholar, precise in his phrases, perhaps even a little formal in conversation, but always frank in his opinions. . . . He was a simple man; but there was something strange and alluring about him, an indescribable charm expressed in his voice and manner, and, above all, in his curious smile that was at the same time ironic and sympathetic. How he has ever been described as "inscrutable" or "unresponsive" seems incomprehensible to me; or how anyone could have spent five minutes in his company without realising both the charm and the power of his personality.'[13]

Anatole LeBraz, the Breton scholar: 'He conducts himself with charm and good manners, very amenable mind, slightly shy. His character is open, welcoming. The man does not have that childish standoffishness that has struck me in many of his compatriots.'[14]

Mrs. Alfred North Whitehead: 'There was one young man, shabbily clad, who said almost nothing and coughed dreadfully. After lunch someone took them the rounds of the college, but this young man stayed behind with Alfred and me. And then! Three hours, he talked brilliantly. We hadn't got his name. But after they were gone, we told each other, "No matter who he is, the man is extraordinary".'[15]

John Masefield: 'When I turn over my memories of him, it seems that his grave courtesy was only gay when he was talking to women. His talk to women had a lightness and charm. It was sympathetic; never self-assertive, as the hard brilliant Irish intellect so often is. He liked people to talk to him. He liked to know the colours of people's minds. He liked to be amused. His merriest talk was like playing catch with an apple of banter, which one afterwards ate and forgot.'[16]

And finally, Lady Gregory: 'One never has to rearrange one's mind to talk to him.'[17]

Contrary to what is commonly believed, Synge had a great many women friends, especially after 1894 when he went to the continent. But even at home, one of his closest companions was his cousin Florence Ross, the first of many accomplished women artists from whom he would learn much about painting. When he travelled to Europe in company with his older cousin, a professional musician, he went first to Germany, staying on a river island, Oberwerth, in Coblenz, with a family of six sisters — and when he arrived — twelve other women boarders. 'The von Eickens, whom he had just left,' Mrs. Synge reported to her eldest son Robert, 'have been very kind and pleasant, and he feels as if they were his oldest friends instead of his newest! What a pity that, when thrown among strangers, we only show ourselves as amiable and agreeable and taking everything in good part – while at home we show ourselves sometimes in a very unpleasant aspect, and temper often spoils our comfort, and certainly the comfort of those we live with.'[18] The litany continues: in Paris he met Thérèse Beydon, an art teacher, feminist, something of an anarchist; they began by exchanging language lessons, became close friends, and to her, as he had to Valeska von Eicken, Synge was completely open and free concerning his love for Cherrie and his artistic aspirations. He visited Italy to study art and met a Polish sculptor, Maria Zdanowska, and an English art historian, Hope Rea; they argued religion, philosophy, politics, and they remained lifelong friends. Back in Paris he met, and fell in love with, an American etcher, Margaret Hardon. Even in County Wicklow, where his mother entertained women missionaries home on furlough, if he did not make close friends (and with a few he did), he was remembered as a charming, open, courteous companion.[19] Among his papers are letters from young girls whom he met on Aran, and nurses who attended him during his bouts in hospital; his diaries carry frequent references, expecially during his stay in Paris, to 'at homes' and evenings spent with a great many friends, both men and women. There are no indications of stormy love affairs, impetuous liaisons, and only a few of unrequited passions, but it is abundantly clear that Synge was neither solitary nor morose, and that, when Molly Allgood finally captured, and returned, his mature love, he was, if not an experienced courtier, certainly very much *himself* in the company of women.

It is against this background that we should read the extraordinarily frank, open and intense record of his correspondence with Molly Allgood, with whom he shared a relationship spanning the full range of passions anatomized in *Deirdre of the Sorrows*. And in these nakedly revealing letters – which for some have been too painful an explosion of the idealized dazzling singer of a fabulous Ireland – we recognize the same daring swing between romantic yearning for perfection of life fully attuned to nature and a realistic awareness of its impossibility or, at best, transience; the tension between art and nature, passion and fulfilment, life and illusion; and the essential irony which bridges the two poles of romance and folly.

December 5th, 1906. Surrey. 'I don't know how I have lived so long without you, for you are a part now of every thought and feeling that I have . . . I have opened the end window . . . so that I can see the stars we used to walk about under, a long time ago! All that we feel for each other is so much connected with this divine world, that our particular affection, in a real sense, must be divine also. What is there in life, dear heart, to come near our walks down that winding road from Enniskerry when the stars themselves seemed like little candles, set round our great love that is more priceless than they are. The stillness of this dim room puts me into a sort of dream. Would to God that you were here that I might put my arms round you and feel that the reality and mystery of our love is stronger even than dreams. (I wonder am I writing nonsense? It sounds uncommonly like it)'.[20]

Again, in what begins as a conventional love letter to his *fiancée*, there is that undercutting which does not deny, but rather affirms, settling both on a more solid base. It is from this wide range of companionship, culminating in his successful courtship of Molly, that Synge, once he had found his *métier*, drew his powerful characterizations of women.

NOTES

1 See Andrew Carpenter, 'Synge and Women', *Etudes Irlandaises*, 1979; Joan Templeton, 'Synge's Redeemed Ireland: Woman as Rebel', *Caliban*, 1980; F.A.E. Whelan and Keith N. Hull, ' "There's Talkin for a Cute Woman!": Synge's Heroines', *Eire*, 1980; Almire Martin, 'On Synge's *Riders to the Sea*: Maurya's Passion', *Cahiers du Centre d'Etudes Irlandaises*, 1977; Ellen S. Spangler, 'Synge's *Deirdre of the Sorrows* as Feminine Tragedy', *Eire*, 1977.

2 J.M. Synge, *The Playboy of the Western World*, *Plays Book II*, ed. Ann

Saddlemyer (Oxford University Press, 1968), pp. 101–103. All subsequent quotations from the plays are taken from this edition.

3 Insufficient critical attention has been paid to the ambiguous farce in Act III when the Widow Quin attempts to dress Christy in a woman's skirt, a far cry from the comic hubris of Shawn's loan of clothing in Act II.

4 Synge to Frank Fay, 10 April 1904, quoted in the introduction to *Plays Book I*, p. xx.

5 Synge to Stephen MacKenna, 28 January 1904, Lilly Library, University of Indiana.

6 W. G. Fay and Catherine Carswell, *The Fays of the Abbey Theatre* (Rich and Cowan, 1935), pp. 138–139.

7 Synge to Frederick J. Gregg, 12 September 1907, quoted in the introduction to *Plays, Book II*, p. xxvii.

8 W. B. Yeats, 'The Tragic Theatre,' *Essays and Introductions* (Macmillan, 1961), p. 239.

9 *Letters to Molly: John Millington Synge to Maire O'Neill*, ed. Ann Saddlemyer (Harvard University Press, 1971), p. 67.

10 Andrew Carpenter, 'Synge and Women', p. 99.

11 C[herrie] H. H[oughton], 'John Synge as I Knew Him', *The Irish Statesman*, 5 July 1924, pp. 533–534.

12 John Butler Yeats, 'Synge and the Irish', *Essays Irish and American* (Talbot Press, 1918), p. 61.

13 Louis Esson, 'J.M. Synge: A Personal Note', *Fellowship*, VII, 9 (April 1921), pp. 138–141.

14 Anatole LeBraz, translation of a letter to Maurice Bourgeois, 23 January 1913, quoted in part in Bourgeois, *John Millington Synge and the Irish Theatre* (Constable, 1913), pp. 19 and 65–66.

15 *Dialogues of Alfred North Whitehead* as recorded by Lucien Price (Little, Brown and Co., 1954), p. 107.

16 John Masefield, *John M. Synge: A Few Personal Recollections with Biographical Notes* (Cuala, 1915), p. 5.

17 Lady Gregory, 'Synge', *English Review*, March 1913, p. 556.

18 Mrs. Kathleen Synge to Robert Synge, 29 January 1894, Synge papers, Trinity College, Dublin, Library.

19 *My Uncle John, Edward Stephen's Life of J.M. Synge*, ed. Andrew Carpenter (Oxford University Press, 1974), pp. 128–132, 136.

20 *Letters to Molly*, p. 70.

THE NEW WOMAN AND THE OLD GODDESS: THE SHAPING OF SHAW'S MYTHOLOGY

J. PERCY SMITH

No one now disputes that Bernard Shaw was not only a profoundly religious man but a profoundly religious playwright. A good deal has been written on the subject, though I dare say that few would go quite as far as Joseph Wood Krutch, who remarked in 1962:

Though he never wrote it all down in systematic form, Shaw has at one time or another propounded the parts of what is probably the most inclusive body of doctrine since Thomas Aquinas.[1]

I do not aspire to be the Thomas of Shavianity. Nonetheless, I should like to discuss some aspects of his religion that have yet been little noted, in particular the way in which certain of the themes of the ancient mythologies are reflected in his plays, and not merely reflected but fundamentally embedded in them, informing them, strengthening them philosophically as well as dramatically, sometimes determining the shape that they assume.

In this paper I shall explore one or two of these themes. Before doing so, I want to deal briefly with three matters that tend to disturb one's reflections on Shaw's religion, and to divert them from the central issues. The first is his iconoclasm and frequent anti-ecclesiasticism. He often enough poked fun at the established church and its clergy, and he rejected certain of the dogmas of Christianity – most particularly that of the atonement. Yet he had a high sense of the fundamental importance of worship and of prayer – a sense that he expressed most directly in the little essay *On Going to Church*, in 1896. Second, it is necessary to recognize and take seriously his conception of the theatre as a place of worship. It is easy enough in our time to read about the religious origins of the drama with a complacent sophistication – not to say sophistry – and the comfortable thought that those old rituals were of significance in their way, of course, and are of antiquarian interest, but that we in our own generation are wiser.

Shaw would not have said so. In 1906, looking back over his days as a critic, he said of the theatre:

In my time none of the critics would claim for it, as I claimed for it, that it is as important as the Church was in the Middle Ages and much more important than the Church was in London in the years under review. A theatre to me is a place 'where two or three are gathered together'. The apostolic succession from Eschylus to myself is as serious and as continuously inspired as that younger institution, the Apostolic succession of the Christian Church. . . . [The Theatre ought to] take itself seriously as a factory of thought, a prompter of conscience, an elucidator of social conduct, an armory against despair and dullness, and a temple of the Ascent of man.[2]

Finally, one has to come to terms with Shaw's comic sense and practice: the wit, the absurdities, the buffoonery that so often are his vehicles. To reconcile them with the essentially serious religious thrust of his thought was not easy for Victorians brought up to identify religion with solemnity, nor is it easy for the generations that follow World War II, for whom the comic is to be seen through blasé Freudian spectacles patented by Masters and Johnson, and religion as either blinkered or peripheral. In dealing with Shaw's religious thought as expressed through his plays it is well to keep in mind the legend of the mediaeval juggler who was found in the church, juggling before the altar because that was his way of worshipping. For Shaw there was (or at least there could be) something sacred in laughter, and he would not have disagreed with the suggestion of Mary Barnard that one of the sources of myths may well have been in the sense of fun that primitive man must have had in common with his descendants. It is no denigration of the significance of myths to make that claim. 'By laughter only can you destroy evil without malice, and affirm good fellowship without mawkishness', Shaw wrote.[3]

To those three concerns – Shaw's iconoclasm, his belief in the drama as a vehicle of worship, his perception and use of the comic – let me add another. I am conscious of speaking to an audience that is likely to be mythologically attuned, so to speak, to the thinking of another mythologist, W.B. Yeats. Yeats and Shaw shared much common ground as Irishmen and writers, but their differences were profound. I think it probable that one root of them was a crucial difference between the views that they held of history and mythology; for Yeats perceived time as cyclical, as returning upon itself through those gyres that he adopted as its symbols, where Shaw – perhaps closer in this respect to Christian thinking – perceived time as linear, and life as evolving eternally, continually creative, unreturning, even though its course might sometimes be interrupted, often erratic. I do not wish to overstate the difference; for Yeats, reflecting at one point in *A Vision* on the course of human history, says:

I think of the hunter's age and that which followed immediately as a time when man's waking consciousness had not reached its present complexity and stability.[4]

The waking and growth of man's consciousness was for Shaw the central matter.

I should like now to examine tentatively, and perhaps provocatively, certain mythological themes that arise in Shaw's plays and to consider them in relation to one of his contemporary social concerns: the status of women. Necessarily, I shall refer to only a few of the plays, making no apology for failing to discuss all those that a full development of the subject would demand. (I am thinking especially of the one called *Getting Married*.)

The essence of the matter is contained in the last small episode of *Major Barbara*. Shaw wrote the play in 1905, and the fashioning of its final act caused him enormous and unaccustomed difficulty; indeed, that act continued to make him uncomfortable for the rest of his life. The episode to which I refer is as follows.

Barbara Undershaft, the Salvation Army major, has renounced her adopted mode of Christianity when she learns where the Army got its money; then, dazzled by the clean, modern company town that her father has built with the proceeds of his armament industry, she has returned to the colours, intoxicated by the prospect of doing God's work among people who are clean, healthy, well-fed, and well-paid – and also by the prospect of marrying Adolphus Cusins, whom she kisses rapturously.

My dearest [says Cusins]: consider my delicate health. I cannot stand as much happiness as you can.
BARBARA. Yes: it is not easy work being in love with me, is it? But it's good for you. (*She runs to the shed, and calls, childlike*) Mamma! Mamma! . . . I want Mamma.

After a moment, her mother comes from the munitions shed.

(. . . *Barbara clutches like a baby at her mother's skirt*.)
LADY BRITOMART. Barbara: when will you learn to be independent and to act and think for yourself? I know as well as possible what that cry of 'Mamma, Mamma', means. Always running to me!
SARAH (*touching Lady Britomart's ribs with her fingertips and imitating a bicycle horn*). Pip! Pip!
LADY BRITOMART (*highly indignant*). How dare you say Pip! Pip! to me, Sarah? You are both very naughty children. What do you want, Barbara?
BARBARA. I want a house in the village to live in with Dolly. (*Dragging at the skirt*) Come and tell me which one to take.

Before this moment the play as it has progressed has focused increasingly, especially in the final act, on Barbara's father, Andrew Undershaft. He is a monumental figure, indeed a Dionysian figure, who intoxicates and overpowers those around him by his presence and force and the wine of his rhetoric (not to mention his money), just as Dionysus overpowered the citizens of Thebes. I have elsewhere examined Shaw's use of Euripides' *The Bacchae* in *Major Barbara* and shall not do so here.* Let me say only that the role of Undershaft combines the role of Euripides' Dionysus with that of Dioscorus, the father of Saint Barbara. As the play ends, he emerges as the towering and magnetic figure who has achieved everything that he wanted.

And yet – and yet – consider for a moment those other two figures, the daughter and the mother, who embody a moment in a process that was going on in the mind of G.B.S., whether or not he was conscious of it. For behind Barbara Undershaft, who in the fashion of the New Woman at the turn of the century (at least as Shaw fancied her) has defied her parents and affirmed her individuality before the world as to marriage, religion, and social class, stands the figure of an early Christian martyr. Saint Barbara, whose legend Shaw certainly knew, had also defied her rich and powerful father on those counts and had been tortured and killed for doing so. Behind the third-century saint was a more shadowy figure still; for the legend is thought to have entered Italy from farther east, and the saint herself has been discredited.

In the legend, the mother of Saint Barbara is not mentioned. Shaw, however, provides his Barbara with one: the formidable Lady Britomart. Her concern for her children, the marrying of her daughters, the succession to the Undershaft fortune, opens the play. She has summoned her long-absent husband to confer with her – and he has obeyed. As the play proceeds, only she can reduce him to abashed silence when he is in full rhetorical flight. And it is she who, the marriages and the succession having been arranged, rules complacently over the final episode, as we have seen – even if her husband is for once allowed the last word.

And what's her history? She is of course a Shavian version of Wilde's Lady Bracknell; but, as her name makes clear, she is much more than that. For behind Lady Brit stands a figure older that Saint Barbara: Britomartis of Crete. It is uncertain whether Britomartis was huntress or protectress or both, and whether or not she was identical with the other Cretan goddess, Dictynna. What is clear is

*See, for example, 'Shaw's Own Problem Play: *Major Barbara*', in *English Studies in Canada*, IV, 4 (Winter, 1978), pp. 450–467. [Editor's note]

that she was one of the forms of the ancient goddess of fertility and wild nature, among whose duties was the care and nurture of children. The Greeks regarded her as the Cretan daughter of Zeus, and hence a half-sister of Dionysus; but she was older that Zeus. R.W. Hutchinson warns against the temptation to identify her with 'the great mother goddess whom the Phrygians so appropriately addressed as "MA" '.[5] I bow to Hutchinson's authority, but it seems rather a pity, especially since Shaw would not have troubled about the distinction. It is of course possible that he picked up the name Britomart from Spenser, who got it from Ariosto and whose Britomart is clearly related to the Artemis of Greek mythology, a later figure than the mother goddess. It is equally probable that it came to him by way of Gilbert Murray, whose influence on the writing of *Major Barbara* was considerable, or of Arthur Evans and others who were exploring the remains of ancient Cretan civilization in the 1890's and early 1900's. In any case Britomartis was, if one sets aside Hutchinson's necessary historical literalism, one of the many ancient manifestations of the ubiquitous maternal divinity, mother of gods, nurturer of the earth and humanity, who is the subject of Robert Graves's *The White Goddess*.

The question whether Shaw, as he wrote *Major Barbara*, was consciously celebrating the ancient mother goddess is, I think, immaterial. It is true that he was one of the most 'conscious' of artists in respect of his materials and the intent with which he used them. On the other hand, he was profoundly aware of the ways in which forces that are beyond the reaches of our conscious minds affect the artist's work, and in the long run determine its final shape and force.

... The existence of a discoverable and perfectly definite thesis in a poet's work by no means depends on his own intellectual consciousness of it,[6]

he had written in 1891 as he contemplated the plays of Ibsen. And proceeding to expound Ibsenism as seen by a Fabian Socialist, he wrote of the long growth of human consciousness in a manner suggestive of Erich Neumann's approach to that subject sixty years later.

... As Man grows through the ages, he finds himself bolder by the growth of his ... spirit ... and dares more and more to love and trust instead of to fear and fight. But his courage has other effects: he also raises himself from mere consciousness to knowledge by daring more and more to face facts and tell himself the truth,[7]

Shaw wrote. Neumann (who like C.G. Jung seems never to have referred to Shaw) was to write,

The evolution of consciousness as a form of creative evolution is the peculiar achievement of Western man. Creative evolution of ego consciousness means that, through a continuous process stretching over thousands of years, the conscious system has absorbed more and more unconscious contents and progressively extended its frontiers.[8]

Shaw, one recognizes, was here focusing on social institutions, Neumann on the phenomena of depth psychology; Shaw was to become interested in exploring the underlying creative force – the Will, the Life Force – while Neumann's interest was in the evolutionary process and its manifestations. The basic conception of man as the product of a process of creative evolution that moves collectively (that is, socially) and individually through stages of increasing consciousness is common to both. Indeed, Neumann at one point in his introduction echoes precisely Shaw's particular social concern, though he gives it a narrower application:

The creativity of consciousness may be jeopardized by religious or political totalitarianism, for any authoritarian fixation of the canon leads to sterility of consciousness.[9]

When Shaw wrote the *Quintessence*, the word 'totalitarianism' had not yet appeared in the language. A follower of Carlyle, Ruskin, and Morris, and a close practical observer, he saw just that sterility of consciousness to which Neumann was to refer – saw it as the product of the various Victorian tyrannies that he assaulted: the tyranny of marriage and of the family, and the tyranny of social class; the blinding tyranny of wealth and the grinding tyranny of poverty; the tyranny of man over woman.

His crusading on behalf of the New Woman, who could be expected to emerge only as society allowed women to be equal with men, continued throughout his life through speeches and essays and such books as *The Intelligent Woman's Guide to World Socialism and Capitalism*. That did not of course mean that he was unaware of the comic side of some of the excesses and illogicalities of the feminist movement. These became – in *The Philanderer* and *You Never Can Tell*, for example, and later in his farcical treatment of the suffragettes in *Press Cuttings* – grist to his dramatic mill. All the same, even when he was urging most energetically the cause of sexual equality, he was beginning to explore the growing perception that the search for sexual equality contains a kernel of incongruity, since the most fundamental creative urge, the Life Force, is itself feminine though it proceeds through both male and female and finds expression in both. What Goethe callled the Eternal Feminine works in ways beyond consciousness to shape human life and destiny, and is the over-arching subject of mythology – being creative, life-giving, nurturing, in a word maternal, as Britomartis was in Crete and is in *Major Barbara*.

Shaw's dramatic study of the force and its process may be said to have begun with *Candida*, which he wrote in 1895. You will recall that in that play a young, naïve, and indeed somewhat silly poet named Marchbanks enters the household of a socialist clergyman called Morell and falls in love with Morell's wife, Candida. He launches an attack on Morell and on the Morell marriage so devastating as to bring about a situation in which Candida must choose between her preaching windbag of a husband and the ardent and perceptive young poet. She chooses Morell, and Marchbanks goes out into the night – 'Tristan's holy night', Shaw called it – to fulfil his poetic mission, having learned that life is nobler than domesticity allows, the fireside dreams less important than the starlit ones. (This superficially comfortable ending may explain why *Candida* has been one of the most frequently performed of Shaw's plays, and also why nobody really likes it.)

In part, *Candida* embodies Shaw's rejoinder to Ibsen's *A Doll's House*, making the point that in many a household it is the husband who is the doll, not the wife. But his intention went much further than that, as one recognizes by reflecting on the woman who gives the play its name. It is incidentally interesting that Shaw said he got the name from an Italian countess, and of course it may be so. But there were several saints named 'Candida', and in the parish church of Whitchurch (that is, White Church) Canonicorum, in West Dorset, are the relics and shrine of the mysterious Anglo-Saxon woman Saint Wite, who was killed by the Danes, and who two or three centuries later, perhaps as a result of etymological confusion, was informally rechristened 'Candida' – the Latin word for 'white'.

In any case, Shaw's intention with regard to his heroine is clear enough: she is the Madonna, the Eternal Mother. In his first brief description of her in the manuscript of the play he called her 'a true Virgin Mother', and had Morell's secretary say of her,

One would think she was the Queen of Heaven herself. [Morell] is thinking of her half the time when he imagines that he is meditating on the virtues of Our Blessed Lady.

Shaw deleted both these passages from the final version, undoubtedly for the sake of public acceptability, not because he changed his mind about her. 'I *have* written THE Mother Play', he wrote to Ellen Terry;[10] and to William Archer, 'Candida . . . is a mother first, a wife twenty-seventh, and nothing else'.[11] To Janet Achurch he wrote of 'the heroine of a play as black as Candida is white'[12] and of 'the religion which rediscovers God in man and the Virgin Mother in every carpenter's wife . . . the most recreative of all religions'.[13] Candida has provided her husband with two children, and when Shaw refers to her as the Virgin Mother he is using the title in the sense of the ancient myths, where virginity was nothing so trifling as a physiological condition. Candida cares nothing about it, nor about marital fidelity, as she makes quite clear.

The Great Mother [wrote Erich Neumann in the book from which I have already quoted] is a virgin . . . in a sense other than that intended by the patriarchate, which later misunderstood her as the symbol of chastity. Precisely in virtue of her fruitfulness she is a virgin, that is, unrelated, and not dependent upon any man.[14]

Candida is indeed a mother to her two children, but she is also a mother to Morell and to Marchbanks, sustaining the former as, in his own words about her,

my wife, my mother, my sisters . . . the sum of all loving care to me;

and wisely, as the nurturing mother, seeing the young poet through the painful process of maturation and self-discovery until he is ready to fly on his own wings.

How far Shaw's conscious intention went, to what extent the play may have been moulded by unconscious or sub-conscious forces, it is of course impossible to tell. That Candida points forward to the later manifestation of the White Goddess, Lady Britomart, is surely clear. Both plays deal with the maternal aspect of that mythological figure. Between them in Shaw's career as playwright came one, in some respects the greatest, of his plays, that celebrated the Great Goddess in a different mode.

For clearly if the Goddess is to be maternal she must first be impregnated: she must be the divinity that inspires sexual love in men, the siren who draws them to her. At this point one might look for the appropriate stage direction: Enter the Snake. And indeed the snake does enter in the first Act of *Man and Superman*, when the heroine – a woman to make men dream, says Shaw in describing her, one in whom vitality rises to the level of genius – enters wearing a boa which she throws playfully around the neck of the man whom she intends to marry. She withdraws it, but the action of the comedy centres on the ways in which she increases and tightens the coils of her allurement around the brilliant chatterbox who is her victim. Her name, Ann Whitefield (can it be coincidence merely?) combines that of another saint, a maternal one, the mother of Mary, with the suggestion of whiteness. At this point I remind myself uncomfortably of C.S. Lewis's wry but salutary remark, recorded by R.S. Loomis, that he had been led to doubt 'whether it is possible for the wit of man to devise anything in which the wit of some other man cannot find, and plausibly find, an allegory'.[15] Before the white Candida among Shaw's women characters was Blanche Trefusis, in *Widowers' Houses*; and after Ann Whitefield there comes Jennifer in *The Doctor's Dilemma*, who comes from Cornwall, where much of the Arthurian legend is set, and whose name, the Cornish form of Guinevere, means 'white spirit'. For her, moreover, certain knights of the medical profession – of the operating table, one might say – are the source of much dule and teen.

Whether or not Shaw intended Ann Whitefield's name to carry a particular reference, there is no doubt about her personifying the Eternal Feminine in its phase of courtship, in the play proper. There he interweaves the fertility motif of the Great Goddess with one of two legends that have virtually risen to the status of myth, that between them depict the plight of post-Renaissance Western man as he asserts his claim to intellectual and moral freedom: the Faust legend and the Don Juan legend. Both fascinated Shaw, the latter particularly as dealt with by Mozart; but unlike other writers and composers who treated it, Shaw saw it in relation to the insistent claims of the Eternal Feminine. Ann Whitefield takes for her victim John Tanner, a man with a touch of 'Olympian majesty' that would 'suggest Jupiter rather than Apollo', of whom Don Juan is a 'famous ancestor'. Tanner is only too conscious of their respective roles and his own fate as the play draws to its close, saying to Ann despairingly,

. . . at the supreme moment the Life Force endows you with every quality.
. . . The trap was laid from the beginning!
ANN (*concentrating all her magic*): From the beginning – from our childhood – for both of us – by the Life Force.
TANNER: I will not marry you. I will not marry you.
ANN: Oh, you will, you will.
TANNER: I tell you, no, no, no.
ANN: I tell you, yes, yes, yes.

and then, Ann, having for the moment lost her courage, says, 'Well, I made a mistake. You do not love me.' To which, in one of those reversals that Shaw knew so well how to effect, Tanner responds by seizing her in his arms, exclaiming,

It is false. I love you, The Life Force enchants me. I have the whole world in my arms when I clasp you.

And so on.

Every romantic comedy comes to that moment of acceptance and union of hearts. What marks the Shavian comedy is the stated recognition that the force at work is cosmic and purposeful and that it is feminine, filling women, not simply with magnetic vitality, but with an intuitive wisdom which the male intellect, no matter how brilliant it may be, cannot match. Moreover, the purpose of the Goddess – or, as Tanner calls her, the Life Force – is not mere procreation, the continuance of the race. It is the promotion of the extension of consciousness to which I earlier referred. In Shaw's view, that extension depends on two devices, one of which is dealt with in the great 'Hell Scene' that comprises the Third Act of *Man and Superman*: the further biological evolution of the human race. The cry of Dona Ana to the universe as the scene ends – 'I believe in the Life to Come! ... A father! a father for the Superman!' – expresses simultaneously and passionately Shaw's recognition that mankind as it is is not good enough and his faith in the creative power and purpose of the Great Goddess: the Life Force. The other device is that of the artist (in this case, the poet), whose function it is to extend our consciousness not through the biological continuing of the race but through a process that is essentially educational.

Ordinary men [Shaw wrote in the Preface to this play] cannot produce really impressive art-works. Those who can are men of genius: that is, men selected by Nature to carry on the work of building up an intellectual consciousness of her own instinctive purpose. Accordingly, we observe in the man of genius all the unscrupulousness and all the 'self-sacrifice' (the two things are the same) of Women ...
... What is true of the great man who incarnates the philosophic consciousness of Life and the Women who incarnate its fecundity is true in some degree of all geniuses and all women.

Incidentally, Shaw allows for the case in which an individual is both genius and woman: 'then the game is one for a king of critics'.

Shaw dealt again with the role of the artist when he wrote his Preface to *Back to Methuselah*, two decades after *Man and Superman*. If one conceives time as linear and life as evolving through the extension of consciousness, one may expect that as the extension proceeds the nature of myths, if not the need, will change. Myths of the sun gods and the sea gods, for example, may diminish to the level of interesting stories as telescopes and spectroscopes and space observatories enlarge our knowledge of the physical cosmos and our relation to it. That does not mean that they may not retain psychological significance, nor does it mean that the significance of the unconscious – collective and individual – is diminished. It may well mean that the forms through which the unconscious is raised to the level of consciousness, made accessible to it and discussible by it, will change. The profound mysteries and miracles of life and consciousness, death and rebirth, remain: the language that mediates between them and our common sensory and intellectual experience, the iconography (to use Shaw's word), changes. The role of the great artist, then, is to provide the new iconography – to show us not merely what we have become but what we must become.

So, in essence, Shaw's argument runs. And in *Back to Methuselah* he set out deliberately to provide a mythology suited to a religion of Creative Evolution in an age of science: to provide a mythological vehicle for dealing with the continuing mysteries of life, consciousness, death, rebirth, and life's origins and purpose. It is an enormous and markedly uneven dramatic corpus and I do not propose to discuss it at length here; but obviously one cannot talk about the shaping of Shaw's mythology and ignore this central, and in a sense climactic, work.

Shaw called the opening section *In the Beginning*, and the phrase suggests the Biblical story that he was to adapt. It is, however, misleading; for the Book of Genesis opens with the words, 'In the beginning God created . . .' and proceeds – as every mythology must – to a myth of creation. To find Shaw's myth of creation, one has to go first to the end of *Back to Methuselah*, to the splendid final speech in which the Great Goddess, in her ultimate Shavian form as the embodiment of the Life Force, the mother of all life, says, giving herself a name,

I am Lilith:
I brought Life into the whirlpool of force, and compelled my enemy, Matter, to obey a living soul.

If now we turn back to the opening section of the drama, we find the serpent in the garden explaining to Eve:

I am old. I am the old serpent, older that Adam, older than Eve. I remember Lilith, who came before Adam and Eve . . . She was alone: there was no man with her. She saw death as you saw it when the fawn fell; and she knew

then that she must find out how to renew herself and cast the skin like me.
She had a mighty will . . . She strove and strove and willed and willed . . .
And when she cast the skin, lo! there was not one new Lilith but two . . .
You were the one: Adam was the other.

Lilith, then, although even in that primordial state she was
feminine, resembles that hermaphroditic figure that in many
mythologies symbolizes the primal unity. Shaw makes no real
attempt to deal with the primal unity, however: the serpent seems to
have been as old as Lilith, and more aggressively imaginative; and
life and matter were separate and at enmity at the earliest point of
Shaw's myth.

The serpent, which in the form of Ann Whitefield's boa as well as
in the scene in Eden was a symbol of sexual force, has a place in
many creation myths. It symbolizes the male principle and the
principle of renewal, a notion that Shaw partly adopts in having the
serpent instruct not only Eve, but by implication Lilith herself, in
the secret of regeneration. Yet it embodies a kind of dualism; for it
is also a symbol of destruction, the enemy of gods and men, as in the
Nordic myths. The dualism offers no difficulty for the creative
evolutionist, of course: destruction is a necessary concomitant of
growth. Shaw, in short, makes no effort to deal with the supreme
mystery of creation itself: unity has already become duality when
his myth begins. He seems content to leave the question where that
strange artist Althea Gyles, for a time the friend of Yeats, left it in
the drawing that she called *Lilith*: the naked woman lying prone, the
serpent on the ground beside her.

In the Beginning, then, develops through the myth of the Garden
and its early inhabitants the themes that are taken up – with a good
deal of tedium at times – in the ensuing sections. The accidental
death of a young fawn leads to the recognition by Adam and Eve
that life must discover how to renew itself, and the Serpent comes
with its knowledge and subtlety to provide the first of all courses in
sex education; but it also shows how the development of language
makes for the extension of consciousness. Man the male learns to
love death: Cain, through the excitement of violence; Adam,
through the discouragement of being obliged to go on digging the
soil forever, never to rest beneath it. The Serpent has taught Adam
to know fear, and in him fear is greater than hope – as he says,
Tithonus-like, to Cain:

I have known what it is to sit and brood under the terror of eternity, of
immortality. Think of it, man: to have no escape! to be Adam, Adam,
Adam through more days than there are grains of sand by the two rivers,

and then be as far from the end as ever! . . . Be thankful to your parents, who enabled you to hand on your burden to new and better men, and won for you an eternal rest; for it was we who invented death.

In Eve, however, hope is stronger than fear, and is linked with imagination as well. And the section ends with her saying,

Man need not always live by bread alone. There is something else. We do not yet know what it is; but some day we shall find out; and then we shall live on that alone; and there shall be no more digging nor spinning, nor fighting nor killing.

Eve embodies the spirit of the Goddess, and it is through her that the evolution of life and purpose proceeds in the remaining sections of *Back to Methuselah*. 'You are Eve,' says Conrad Barnabas to his niece Savvy, in the second Section of the play; 'The Eternal Life persists . . . You are only a new hat and frock on Eve.' The Goddess is embodied too in Mrs. Lutestring, in Part III, with her 'Dianesque' appearance and her vitality, and her two hundred and seventy-four years. Finally, in Part V, she appears again at the last as Lilith herself, to reflect on the course of creative evolution up to the year 31920 A.D. and to consider, still with hope, the future. For Shaw's mythology could not conceivably end in a blaze of cosmic destruction, even though in *Heartbreak House*, which he wrote not long before *Back to Methuselah*, he faltered in that direction. Not for him a Twilight of the Gods – no matter how thrillingly Wagner might have declared for it – but rather the voice of Lilith saying,

Of Life only is there no end; and though of its million starry mansions many are empty and many still unbuilt, and though its vast domain is as yet unbearably desert, my seed shall one day fill it and master its matter to its uttermost confines.

Twenty-five years after writing *Back to Methuselah*, Shaw, eighty-eight years old, wrote what he called a Postscript, actually an introduction to the World Classics edition of the play. There he again discussed the function of art as that of embodying through images ideas that would be unacceptable, even heretical, if boldly stated.

. . .Heretical teaching must be made irresistibly attractive by fine art if the heretics are not to starve or burn,

he observed. He might have been echoing the words of Sallustius, writing two thousand years earlier:

To wish to teach the whole truth about the Gods to all produces contempt in the foolish, because they cannot understand, and lack of zeal in the good; whereas to conceal the truth by myths prevents the contempt of the foolish, and compels the good to practise philosophy.[16]

'She hath built up life from her own body', said the worshippers of the ancient Egyptian mother goddess. In *Back to Methuselah* Shaw spells out the renewal that is implicit in virtually all his plays, through the mother goddess who builds up life. What strikes one as fresh in his mythology is his passionate conviction that the life that is built up has a purpose and a direction. The Eternal Return, the ever-recurring cycle, may indeed include resurrection, but the resurrection is merely the necessary first step to another death. Shaw would have found little to choose between such an hypothesis and the mindless universe that seemed to him, as to Samuel Butler, implicit in the Darwinian version of evolution. The Eternal Feminine draws us *onwards*, says Goethe, and his word *hinan* suggests upwards as well.

There is not time here to examine further implications of his mythology, or to consider that groups of plays after *Back to Methuselah* that one critic has called 'eschatological'. However (since I gave this paper a title before I began writing it), let me make two further observations. I think it was not just a coincidence that Shaw wrote *Saint Joan* almost immediately after *Back To Methuselah* and found the writing of it virtually effortless, as he himself testified. For if the eternal principle of life, the Life Force, is feminine, and if her shaping, continuing purpose is the extension of consciousness, then it is hardly surprising that the genius who leads in breaking through those periods of sterility of consciousness to which I earlier referred, and undertakes the role of heretic, should sometimes be a woman, or that she should be destroyed in the process. For all his essentially comic perception, Shaw had been drawn to the figure of the female martyr long before he wrote about Joan. Barbara Undershaft is, like her namesake before her, a religious martyr, except that her creator lets her off by a specious recantation that permits her to serve God with her eyes blindfolded. Lavinia, in *Androcles and the Lion*, is given a more honest treatment, coming to the point where she recognizes that the martyr does not go to her death for the sake of heaven, or for stories or dreams. 'But for what?' asks the young Roman captain.

LAVINIA. I don't know. If it were for anything small emough to know, it would be too small to die for. I think I'm going to die for God. Nothing else is real enough to die for.

But Lavinia, thanks to Androcles and his friendly lion, escapes the brutality of the arena and will continue to 'strive for the coming of the God who is not yet'. By the time that he had written *Methuselah*, Shaw had accepted that the fact and nature of martyrdom, its cruelty and ugliness, had to be faced by him if his mythology were to carry artistic conviction, his iconography to be complete. The hard truth had to be recognized, that some manifestations of the Great Goddess must become sacrifices to her continuing purpose. Joan of Arc, whose story had haunted Shaw's mind for many years, was the inevitable vehicle of his dramatic and mythological purpose.

Saint Joan, in effect, essentially completes the shaping of Shaw's mythology. In the plays that followed it he is engaging largely in political and social comment, though he sometimes reverts to mythological devices. He does not return to declaring and exploring the purposes of the Great Goddess. That does not necessarily mean that he had lost faith in them; but he was growing old, and the ways of the 1920's and 1930's were not the ways of the New Woman as he had optimistically thought of her in the decade before World War I. As A.H. Nethercot remarked,

As Shaw got older the New Woman seemed to him to get younger, narrower, and brasher. He followed her with eager interest and endowed her with many of his own favorite ideas, but a note of asperity began to creep into his characterizations, and this annoyance deepened into a positive distaste as the gap between her generation and his widened.[17]

Her freedom from Victorian tyranny had not transformed her into a noticeably better vehicle for the purposes of creative evolution. In *Too True to be Good*, for example, the young patient, who has been rescued from respectability and family oppression and all the other tyrannies, turns on her rescuer after some experience of liberty and says:

If I do nothing but contemplate the universe there is so much in it that is cruel and terrible and wantonly evil, and so much more that is oppressively astronomical and endless and inconceivable and impossible, that I shall just go stark raving mad and be taken back to my mother with straws in my hair. The truth is, I am free; I am healthy; I am happy; and I am utterly miserable.

She was speaking for a generation that had achieved an ancient goal – individual freedom – and now did not know what to do with it or what was the goal beyond that one.

Nethercot looked at the significance of some of the names Shaw gave to his characters, including the mythological reference of Britomartis that I have noted, though he did not enlarge on it.

Coming to deal with Shaw's last exuberantly female character, the heroine of *The Millionairess* (a play written by Shaw when he was almost eighty), Nethercot mused on her name: Epifania Ognisanti di Parerga – a Portuguese agglomeration, of sorts. He said,

Her Christian names seem to mean 'Revelation All-Holy' – a more or less prophetic selection by her parents in view of her own evaluation of herself.[18]

But to say only that much is to ignore the surname 'Parerga'. A parergon is something aside from or supplementary to the main purpose – a mere embellishment. Shaw's use of the word is capable of more than one interpretation, and perhaps that is why he provided a kind of desperate alternative ending to *The Millionairess*, in which Epifania speaks exuberantly of what life would be for her if only she were in Communist (at that time Stalinist) Russia – how she would devote her energies and her entire being to the cause of human betterment there:

I shall not be an empress; and I may work myself to death; but in a thousand years from now holy Russia shall again have a patron saint, and her name shall be Saint Epifania.

When in response her husband-to-be suggests that the British Empire be made a Soviet republic, she exclaims:

By all means; but we shall have to liquidate all the adult inhabitants and begin with the newly-born. And the first step to that is to get married.

It sounds like a faint, despairing echo of Dona Ana's cry for a father for the superman, and I should not care to attach great significance to a brief alternative ending that was appended to a late play in the certain knowledge that it would never be utilized. Yet I wonder whether it does not provide a final touch in the shaping of Shaw's mythology at a point where it intersects, so to speak, his sociology. For the competitive social system of free enterprise, Shaw might well have argued, is like the ancient hunting society – essentially a male invention that favours the Andrew Undershafts of this world, promotes inequality, and is in the long run inimical to the creative purposes of the White Goddess, the Life Force. Somewhere (though surely not in Russia at present!), some day, the sort of social, religious, and biological revolution that will make them possible will occur. Certainly in England the New Woman had not evinced any comprehension of that eternal goal. But then, neither had the Old Man.

NOTES

1 J.W. Krutch, *'Modernism' in Modern Drama* (New York, 1962), p. 50.
2 Bernard Shaw, *Our Theatres in the Nineties* (Standard Edition, 1932), p. vi.
3 *Ibid*.
4 W.B. Yeats, *A Vision* (London, 1937), p. 206.
5 R.W. Hutchinson, *Prehistoric Crete* (Penguin, 1962), p. 206.
6 Bernard Shaw, 'The Quintessence of Ibsenism', in *Major Critical Essays* (Standard Edition, 1932), p. 12.
7 *Ibid*., p. 25.
8 Erich Neumann, *The Origins and History of Consciousness*, trs. R.F.C. Hull (Princeton, 1954), p. xviii.
9 *Ibid*., p. xix.
10 Bernard Shaw, *Collected Letters: 1874–1897*, ed. Dan H. Laurence (London, 1965), p. 641.
11 Bernard Shaw, *Collected Letters: 1898–1910*, ed. Dan H. Laurence (London, 1972), p. 137.
12 *Letters: 1874–1897*, p. 472.
13 *Ibid*., p. 505.
14 Neumann, p. 52.
15 R.S. Loomis, *The Development of Arthurian Romance* (London, 1963), p. 164.
16 Quoted in Gilbert Murray, *Five Stages of Greek Religion* (Oxford, 1925), p. 192.
17 A.H. Nethercot, *Men and Supermen* (Cambridge, Mass., 1954), p. 108.
18 *Ibid*., p. 295.

'TWO WORDS FOR WOMEN': A REASSESSMENT OF O'CASEY'S HEROINES

RONALD AYLING

I

In many ways my appointed task would seem to be unnecessary, if it is not a sinecure; surely by now we know O'Casey's heroines and have a pretty shrewd idea from his writings of his attitude to women in general? Moreover, with two bulky volumes of his *Letters* now in print and with the fairly recent testimony of his widow in her two autobiographical books, we now have reliable first-hand information regarding his relationships with several women in particular. Indeed, have we not known his standpoint on this matter all along? From very early in his playwriting career, critics and reviewers of his first staged plays saw an essential dichotomy in his work: on the one hand, there were the long-suffering Dublin slum women representing the creative forces in society, the forces that make for life or enhance and protect life, and, on the other hand, there were the men – virtually without exception irresponsible and self-centred – representing those elements in life and organised society that make for strife and anarchy, discord and war, or (when not directly responsible for, say, death and disorder) nonetheless standing for elements that either make existing evils worse or make their banishment or alleviation much more difficult to effect. The women of O'Casey's early Dublin plays – *The Shadow of a Gunman*, *Juno and the Paycock*, *Nannie's Night Out* and *The Plough and the Stars*, especially – were, from the very first, seen as life-enhancing and the men as actually or potentially destructive and life-crippling.

It still seems difficult to quarrel with this general stress in the earliest criticisms of his Abbey plays, though – as we shall see – several contemporary critics have taken pot shots at it, though only one (Jack Mitchell) has made a serious attempt to undermine it fundamentally.[1] A.E. Malone, the first historian of the Abbey Theatre movement, epitomized the orthodox attitude as follows:

Juno and the Paycock has its superficial qualities, but it is uplifted and ennobled by the character of Juno. Juno is the great, the universal mother, as great as the greatest mother in drama, even though her influence be limited to two rooms in a Dublin slum . . . Her son dead 'for his country'; her daughter betrayed by a worthless liar and deserted by a braggart coward; her husband a boasting, lying, drunken wastrel; she rises superior to her slum surroundings and prepares to begin her life-struggle anew.

It is difficult to argue against this, however much the overheated style may make one wince, however much one may disagree with Malone's judgement elsewhere in his critique that the Abbey dramas are 'all "slices of life" in the strictest and most literal sense of the term', or however much one would prefer a different critical emphasis from his view that these plays 'depend for their significance upon personalities'. Of *Juno and the Paycock*, he asserts:

'Patriotism is not enough,' this play shouts with Nurse Cavell, and the audience laughs at the drunken antics of Boyle and Daly! Sacrifices are made for, and in the name of, the Motherland, but the mother of flesh and blood is spurned, derided, sacrificed, or ignored! Ireland, the Motherland, is loved as an abstraction; Juno is compelled to live in a slum, to see her children sacrificed, but she is ignored because she is merely a reality. Even her own son will fight for the abstraction instead of working for his mother!

Malone's summary of *The Plough* continues this line of argument:

The shattering of dreams and the survival of communities seems to be the theme of *The Plough and the Stars* . . . Death, destruction, suffering, waste; all in the sacred name of patriotism! Again it is the women who suffer, the women who are great. 'Is there anybody goin' with a titther o' sense?' asks the consumptive child. The men talk and dream, loot and die for their dreams; the women live and die for the realities.

So much for A.E. Malone, himself not a good critic but a fair representative of O'Casey's first commentators.

In the majority of slum families it is the women that suffer most, as O'Casey knew from personal experience. While the men escape from their homes to the tavern (or, if employed, to their jobs), the women are left to look after the children. Juno and Mary are at home when the removal men arrive to take away the furniture that the Boyle family had obtained on hire-purchase terms; the head of the household, meanwhile, is dead-drunk in a local 'snug'. At the end of Act I of *The Plough*, Nora Clitheroe is left alone in her tenement home with the consumptive child Mollser; the rest of the inhabitants of the tenement have gone off to booze, whore and to attend a mass political demonstration. The women work hard for the sake of their children, performing miracles of thrift and displaying considerable physical bravery. They bear a major portion of the burdens and hardship and anxiety, as Juno Boyle tells her son:

Who has kep' th' home together for th' past few years – only me? An' who'll have to bear th' biggest part o' this throuble but me? – but whinin' an' whingin' isn't goin' to do any good.

In such speeches O'Casey acknowledges the responsible role of women in slum society, and his dramatic realisation of their self-sacrifice and heroism is well known to be one of the more memorable aspects of his work.

The creativity and life-enhancement of the tenement women are not confined to material self-sacrifice or domestic management. In their outward vivacity and sheer enjoyment of life, the young women embody (in however restricted a capacity) aesthetic values and spiritual qualities that offer, temporarily, resilience and resistance to the drabness and deadening routine of slum conditions. The sensitivity of the young women in O'Casey's plays is shown most clearly in their dress sense: this factor is clearly noted in the stage directions and is also skilfully emphasised in the course of the dramatic action. However trivial they may seem, Minnie's pompoms, Mary's ribbons, and Nora's new hat are all outward and visible signs of an inward and spiritual aesthetic sense. Many men look upon feminine concern for dress and physical appearance as vanity and frivolity, even though they may take pride in the appearance of their wives. More perceptively, O'Casey projects these qualities as the natural and, often, the only possible expression of the latent artistic sense of the tenement women. In such ways, he may truly be said not only to embody an heroic spirit in the characters of his heroines – a commonplace observation in O'Casey criticism, of course – but to view the world from the woman's point of view as well. His identification with this most downtrodden portion of the proletariat, and its needs and desires, is shown to advantage in sensitive short stories like 'The Job' and 'The Star-Jazzer', where the action is seen through the minds of the women concerned in a way that is virtually impossible in the dramatic *genre*. There are, in his autobiographical writings also, various heightened moments when he looks at the world through the eyes of women or views them with especial compassion and sympathy: most notably, perhaps, in the turbulent stream-of-consciousness soliloquy of his sister immediately before she sets off, alone, to marry despite the vehement opposition of her mother. In 'Hail, Smiling Morn', an early chapter in the first book of autobiography, the playwright enters into the excited self-justifying thoughts and feelings of the intelligent but misguided young woman – and, while no injustice is accorded to her standpoint, the love-blinded self-deceit that attends it is also made apparent. Throughout the autobiographies, indeed, O'Casey's concern and high regard for women is everywhere realised. Highlights include the cumulative build-up of his mother's portrait – an enduring literary achievement – as well as the memorable creation of complete strangers, like Mild Milly in *Drums under the Windows*, who suddenly enter the narrative and, just as abruptly, leave it.

Despite his sympathies for women as the most victimized members of society (and, in particular, proletarian society), O'Casey mostly avoids idealising them inordinately. Certainly, his is not an uncritical portrayal of womankind. One of the more intolerable aspects of slum living for many of the young girls is having to endure the jealous hostility of the older women. Jack Boyle's condemnation of his daughter's attempts towards self-education ('Her an' her readin'! That's more o' th' blasted nonsense that has the house fallin' down on top of us! What did th' like of her, born in a tenement house, want with readin'?') is indicative of inherent tenement hostility against efforts at self-improvement made by members of the slum community. And, though they should be foremost in recognising the spiritual and aesthetic needs of those who are like themselves as they were when young, many of the older tenement women are as narrow-minded and hypocritical as is Boyle. The attempts of Minnie Powell and Nora Clitheroe – in *The Shadow of a Gunman* and *The Plough and the Stars*, respectively – to bring some degree of refinement and taste into their lives in matters of dress and in living habits encounter resentment and jealousy from their neighbours. Mrs. Grigson expresses what seems to be the common feeling about Minnie, when the girl is arrested by the Black and Tans for possessing I.R.A. arms:

The little hussy, to be so deceitful; she might as well have had the house blew up! God to-night, who'd think it was Minnie Powell? . . . With her fancy stockins, an' her pompoms, an' her crepe de chine blouses! I knew she'd come to no good!

As with Minnie, Nora Clitheroe's neighbours are jealous of her dress sense, and suspicious of her air of refinement. Mrs. Gogan's attitude is representative:

God, she's going' to th' divil lately for style! That hat, now, cost more than a penny. Such notions of upperosity she's gettin' (*Putting the hat on her head*) Oh, swank, what! . . . An' th' way she tries to be polite with her 'Good mornin', Mrs. Gogan,' when she's goin' down, an' her 'Good evenin', Mrs. Gogan,' when she's comin' up. But there's politeness an' politeness in it . . .

Oh, you know, she's a well up little lassie, too; able to make a shillin' go where another would have to spend a pound. She's wipin' th' eyes of th' Covey an' poor oul' Pether – everybody knows that – screwin' every penny she can out o' them, in ordher to turn th' place into a baby-house. An' she has th' life frightened out o' them; washin' their face, combin' their hair, wipin' their feet, brushin' their clothes, trimmin' their nails, cleanin' their teeth – God Almighty, you'd think th' poor men were undergoin' penal servitude.

To which charges Fluther makes the not unexpected rejoinder: 'A-a-ah, that's goin' beyond th' beyonds in a tenement house.'

Yet despite active disparagement and opposition, from within their own class as well as from without, there is in the minds of many of the tenement women – before years of grinding poverty and rearing large families wear down their hope and idealism – active desire for a better life and the determination to achieve it. The stage direction which first introduces Mrs. Boyle to the audience clearly makes the point that, at forty-five years of age, she shows signs of the strain that she has borne for many years:

twenty years ago she must have been a pretty woman, but her face has now assumed that look which ultimately settles down upon the faces of the women of the working-class; a look of listless monotony and harassed anxiety, blending with an expression of mechanical resistance.

In the early course of the play she appears to have lost any idealism that she may once have had, yet at the end, when the most testing time occurs, she shows herself still capable of confronting the most difficult of challenges with courage and practical resolution.

More consciously than Minnie or Juno Boyle, Nora Clitheroe battles for her ideas of a better and more sensitive way of life, and though she is mildly criticised by the author (he describes her as one who is 'a little anxious to get on in the world' in a presumably bourgeois sense), there is no doubt that her instincts are basically sound. There is strength as well as sensitivity in her nature: 'The firm lines of her face are considerably opposed by a soft, amorous mouth and gentle eyes. When her firmness fails her, she persuades with her feminine charm', as an early stage-direction in *The Plough and the Stars* indicates. It is well that she possesses such powers for the two relatives who share the flat with her husband and herself are difficult to 'reform', as she points out to them:

Are yous always goin' to be tearin' down th' little bit of respectability that a body's thryin' to build up? Am I always goin' to be havin' to nurse yous into th' hardy habit o' thryin' to keep up a little bit of appearance? . . . If th' two

o' yous don't thry to make a generous alteration in your goins on, an' keep
on thryin' to inaugurate th' customs o' th' rest o' th' house into this place,
yous can flit into other lodgins.

Other speeches by her as well as visual details in the rooms she
has decorated for her enlarged family exhibit her fumbling attempts
to introduce more demanding standards of cleanliness and taste into
the drab and dilapidated tenement. Among other things, we may
notice that, while all the other windows in her 'street of tenements'
are 'grimy' and 'draped with fluttering and soiled fragments of lace
curtains', the two windows belonging to the Clitheroes' apartment
are not only spotless but are 'hung with rich, comparatively, case-
ment cloth'. That is the street, as seen from without, in Act III. From
within the Clitheroes' home, in Act I, we may note the reproduc-
tions of paintings on the wall: they are obviously Nora's acquisitions
and include 'The Sleeping Venus', 'The Gleaners' and 'The
Angelus'. The playwright's endorsement of her taste in this regard
may be guessed from the fact that he himself had a large reproduction of Giorgione's 'The Sleeping Venus' hanging in his own tenement room and retained it in his working study throughout thirty-
eight years of exile in England. An indication that such visual details
are to be regarded as touchstones of moral as well as aesthetic
values among the slum dwellers is shown in the predictably cen-
sorious (if comic) reactions of Mrs. Gogan, Fluther and Peter Flynn to
the nude Venus early in the drama. Having had to struggle against
all the odds to overcome inadequate education and her upbringing,
Nora has developed, however lightly, her aesthetic sense, but the
usual response in tenement society is apathy, ridicule, or puritanical
disapproval – and none of the protesters are more scathing or
backbiting than are the older women in the group.

Of all the women in the early dramas it is Juno Boyle who most
receives and most deserves critical acclaim. Yet even she is sub-
jected to a good deal of unflattering scrutiny in the course of the
action. Though her pragmatic attitude to youthful idealism is understandable, given her economic circumstances, it nonetheless seems
rigidly dogmatic, even cynical on occasion: she does not seem to
recognize *any* ethical validity in the social or political views of her
children. Mary is out on strike in support of a workmate who the
workers think was victimized by the employer. Juno sees no justification for this stand, because Mary had never liked the girl in
question; her view is pronounced without any regard for the rights
or wrongs of the case in question. Similarly, her opposition to
Johnny's active participation in the Irish revolutionary struggle is
enunciated without reference to the moral issues involved. It is true

that, to defend their actions, both her children resort to the self-same vacuous slogan ('a principle's a principle', pronounced without any further intellectual arguments to support their causes), while Juno's attitude in each case is practical, consistent and, invariably, down-to-earth ('you lost your best principle, me boy, when you lost your arm; them's the only sort o' principles that's any good to a workin' man'). Nonetheless, her standpoint is primarily self-interested, and the lack of any underlying ethical or moral values is hardly compatible with the religious beliefs she professes elsewhere in the narrative.

She also has a strongly materialistic outlook and an eye for the main chance (the promotion of Charles Bentham rather than Jerry Devine for the hand of her daughter, for instance) which can be viewed as social-climbing adventurism that also embodies a good deal of snobbery. Indeed, the earliest holograph draft of *Juno and the Paycock* made much more of the bourgeois pretensions and selfishness of Jack and Juno Boyle, and the latter was shown to be as culpable as her husband. Moreover, in this version her indifference towards the children was presented as being no less than his. Changes were made subsequently, so that the published script softens Juno's nature in this respect; other textual alterations were introduced in order to emphasise major faults in the Paycock's character. In the first manuscript version the following exchange between Mary Boyle and the trade union official ('Annie' and 'Jim' in the holograph draft) highlights parental irresponsibility. In this scene the young girl, who is presented in a definitely empathetic manner, makes a strong attack upon both her father and her mother during which she evidently draws little or no distinction between them. Immediately before the ensuing dialogue, the young people have overheard an extremely unpleasant quarrel between Mary's parents:

ANNIE: There is the sort o' scenes that I have to look [on] every mortal day. You're always talkin' about the necessity for betther education for the workingclass kids, but, I'm thinkin', there's a bigger necessity for educatin' the mothers an' fathers, than there is for educatin' kids.

JIM: It's hard right enough, Mary, to have to put up with it, but after all, they are your father and mother, aren't they?

ANNIE: Well, what o' that: it's not a very wonderful thing to have a father an' mother, is it?

JIM: Well, we all know, or ought to know, our duty to our parents.

ANNIE: Oh, I'm sick to death o' the life I'm livin' here! The mother is only able to think of herself, an' me da is only willin' to think of himself. When I'm bringin' in money I'm a help, an' when I'm bringin' in no money I'm a nuisance. That's the long an' short of it.

The material in this scene that was eventually excluded from the final version shows us that when O'Casey began to write the first few scenes of Act I he was less sympathetically inclined towards Juno Boyle, emphasising as he did the clash between the genera- tions and giving Mary good grounds for her strong rebellion against the ignorance and selfishness of *both* her parents. The young girl is obviously attracted towards Bentham (who is given no name in the holograph draft) because he is so different from all those whom she has known hitherto in her environment. Unfortunately, because she is only half educated, she is unable to see that the school-teacher's apparently enlightened ideas and culture are no more than a sophis- ticated veneer. But, although she is incapable of distinguishing between illusion and reality in this case, she is perceptive enough to see through pretension and insincerity within the society with which she herself is familiar. Her rebellion against authority and drab uniformity is emotional and aesthetic as well as intellectual; by contrast, in all the various drafts of the play, Juno buys many vulgar and imposing possessions (presumably to impress her neighbours) once the family appears to receive a legacy. Though sympathetic to the mental anguish of her shell-shocked son, she cannot extend her compassion to other victims of the internecine strife or even towards their grieving parents. Her comments blaming Robbie Tancred's mother for the social 'inconveniences' attending the murdered man's political actions are callous and unfeeling, as we shall subsequently see.

These are insignificant limitations and defects in a character regarded by many critics (of whom A.E. Malone, quoted earlier, is only too representative) as well-nigh perfect. Yet the greatest of her attributes is almost certainly the ability to rise above all her inbred prejudice and selfishness to stand by her daughter in her social disgrace – and no social group will be more condemnatory than the other slum women, particularly as Mary will always have seemed to them to be somewhat 'superior' in dress and manner. For Juno to leave her husband in order to look after daughter and illegitimate grandchild is an act of great courage. Earlier, seen cradling the body of the frightened, crippled Johnny in Act II, Juno is the comforting figure in a *pietà* scene of some power; this is but a symbolic visual foreshadowing of the more demanding role she voluntarily takes on towards the end of Act III when, in the prayer to the Virgin Mary, we see her as worthily representative of suffering womankind and, especially, motherhood. Juno Boyle grows in stature as the situation of her family worsens, in like manner to that of the newly independent nation itself. Juno Boyle is undoubtedly the most important character in the play, the only one to be truly honest with herself and become self-critical in a positive manner.

Though some recent critics (Jack Mitchell, for instance) are reluctant to grant bravery to characters like Minnie Powell, because it appears to them that she is misguided in her loyalties and sense of values, it is impossible to overlook Juno Boyle's tenacious courage: this is seen in her fierce defence of Mary against the Paycock's vicious anger, her plucky resilience in facing a series of bitter blows (including the murder of her son) at the end of the play and, throughout, the aggressive even humorous manner in which she bears the manifold troubles and tribulations of a working tenement mother in a country rent apart by civil war.

Juno has not been destroyed by her environment, as Mrs. Heegan has been, and is seen to be, in *The Silver Tassie*; whereas the latter behaves like an automaton throughout the play in which she appears, Mrs. Boyle rises to each challenge. At the end of *Juno*, in making up her mind to leave Boyle in order to help her daughter and her illegitimate child face a new if arduous life, her attitude is positive as well as clear-sighted: 'I've done all I could [for Boyle] an' it was all no use – he'll be hopeless till the end of his days.' In *Juno and the Paycock* the move is towards a society of women (though there's no evidence that this was the playwright's 'message'), with Juno and Mary staying with Juno's sister until the baby is born. The Ibsen-like or even Syngean conclusion here looks forward to later plays like *Cock-a-Doodle Dandy*, where the young people (men as well as women) are forced to leave at the end of the play in order to make their own way in freedom; there, too, Lorna Marthraun leaves her husband to accompany a daughter who has been turned out of doors by him.

At the close of *Juno*, the mother's courage amid suffering – she has just received word of Johnny's death – brings her closer to her daughter, with whom she has appeared out of touch throughout the earlier period of the play. The terrible news provides one of the climactic moments of truth in the play. Both women respond magnificently: their immediate reaction is to comfort each other – and such selflessness is in marked contrast to the conduct of everyone else in the play when confronted with unpleasant revelations, whether it be the death of Tancred or of Johnny, the failure of the bequest (and here we see the reactions of many of the neighbours as well as those of the members of the family), or Mary's pregnancy. During the course of the action, most of the characters, however minor, are called upon to respond to some such situation, and by their words or actions are themselves judged. They either try to evade responsibility – like Bentham's going to England when he hears that the will is a wash-out, or Devine's spurning Mary when he realises she is pregnant by Bentham – or they seek refuge in self-pity. The reactions of Boyle and Johnny to the revelation about Mary are typical: the former whines, 'Oh, isn't this a nice thing to come on top o' me, an' the state I'm in! A pretty show I'll be to Joxer an' to that oul' wan, Madigan! Amn't I afther goin' through enough without havin' to go through this!' while Johnny exclaims bitterly, 'I've a nice sisther, an' a nice father, there's no bettin' on it. I wish to God a bullet or a bomb had whipped me ou' of this long ago! Not one o' yous, not one o' yous, have any thought for me!' In contrast, Juno's reaction is quite different, when she says to Boyle:

What you an' I'll have to go through'll be nothin' to what poor Mary'll have to go through; for you an' me is middlin' old, an' most of our years is spent; but Mary'll have maybe forty years to face an' handle, an' every wan o' them'll be tainted with a bitther memory.

When Mrs. Boyle receives the news of her son's murder, Mary puts her arm round her and calls out, 'Oh, mother, mother, me poor, darlin' mother.' This shows her genuine love and concern for Juno. More important, it is also a cry of recognition. Divided as these women were earlier in the action by the gulf between the generations, and the distrust it engenders, the young girl's gesture and words here mark a new awareness of their relationship and an acceptance of it. Juno has lost a son but found a daughter. She has had to earn her right to filial love, however, by suffering, self-criticism, and a change in attitude in certain respects. Her compassion and humanity lift her out of the stereotyped moral postures of her generation and class; defying public opinion and the censure that will be rife in tenement society, she elects to stand by Mary whatever the consequence.

Juno's self-criticism at the end of the play corrects a perceptible lapse of charity earlier. I think most spectators will have been horrified when, unaccountably (for she has hitherto shown sympathy for the newly bereaved Mrs. Tancred), Mrs. Boyle says callously:

In wan way, she deserves all she got; for lately, she let the die-hards make an open house of th' place; an' for th' last couple of months, either when th' sun was risin', or when th' sun was settin' you had C.I.D. men burstin' into your room assin' you where.you were born, where were you married, an' where would you be buried!

Taken in conjunction with her lack of sympathy for the idealism of her children, such a speech reveals a failure in human understanding that gives greater depth and even a degree of ambiguity to Juno's character and prevents her from being a wholly admirable (and, possibly, dull) tragic heroine. However, with the death of her own son, Juno comes to realise, painfully, her earlier lack of feeling. Her contrition is deeply felt, reinforced as it is by its context in the play as a whole: 'Maybe I didn't feel sorry enough for Mrs. Tancred when her poor son was found as Johnny's been found now – because he was a Die-hard! Ah, why didn't I remember that then he wasn't a Die-hard or a Stater, but only a poor dead son!'

Though Juno has made mistakes in her family relationship as well as outside them, her basic moral strength and compassion are most clearly evident when the need for them is greatest. She learns from her own sufferings, and by undertaking – without reproach or self-pity – to help Mary, single-handedly, she earns the right to filial love and respect. Serious errors of judgement characterise the actions of daughter and mother during the play; both eventually unite to redeem themselves by disinterested work and possible self-sacrifice on behalf of life yet to come. Like much else in the drama, Juno's final departure is both part of the realistic action of the plot and, at the same time, symbolic – though in this instance the symbolic gesture is one of new-found hope and resolution.

There are, aesthetically, losses as well as gains in the playwright's determination to promote the cause of women or, at least, to portray tenement women like Juno Boyle with especial sympathy. Overly contrived contrasts and an over-insistent thematic emphasis at times betray a didactic strain. Take but one of several loaded moments in these dramas, a line spoken by Mrs. Boyle towards the end of *Juno*: talking to her pregnant unmarried daughter, who has just lamented that the child will have no father, Juno replies crisply with words that could have the force of a clarion call or, at least, a belligerent challenge: 'It'll have what's far betther – it'll have two mothers', meaning herself as well as Mary, of course. This is a declaration of independence, certainly, for her decision to support Mary is taken in conjunction with the resolve that they shall both leave home and her husband, to devote themselves to a new life. It is, arguably, a declaration of sexist superiority, too, for the statement is made in absolute terms: the specific situation to which it refers would hardly be contested by any spectator, for Juno and her daughter will obviously be far better guardians for any child than either Bentham or Boyle (or both) could ever be. However, that two mothers are always better than a mother and a father – and Juno's declaration strongly implies this – is obviously a more debatable proposition.

The positioning of this declaration is all important here: there could not be a more potent scene as framework for it. The line occurs almost immediately before Juno's impassioned prayer that brings her role in the drama to a memorable conclusion; indeed, the statement itself occurs but two short speeches before her final appeal to the Virgin. In such an emotion-charged atmosphere in a climactic scene, the line inevitably has a far greater impact than it would have if it came earlier in the action. That the playwright means the message to have this extra 'charge' is shown, I think, by the contrived verbal manoeuvring at this point. In order for Juno to have the excuse to make her statement, Mary must utter one of the more sentimental lines in the play: 'My poor little child that'll have no father!' Perhaps, in a good stage production, Juno's quick retort ('It'll have what's far bether – it'll have two mothers') would cover up what seems to me to be the falsity of Mary's initial statement: it cannot do so on the page, however, where we see only too sharply that O'Casey has bought an effective piece of propaganda at the expense of Mary's character here.

Though the young girl has faults and can be taken in by the sophisticated veneer of a charlatan like Bentham, Mary Boyle is neither sentimental nor self-pitying elsewhere in the action of the play. Her controlled intellectual repudiation of the double standards in Jerry Devine's morality is made almost immediately before this scene with her mother. She has an immediate retort to the Trade Union leader, who has come pleading to her to resume their relationship now that Bentham has left her – only to change his mind, radically, when he hears she is pregnant. Her response is forthright and unequivocal: 'It's only as I expected – your humanity is just as narrow as the humanity of the others.' In this speech she alludes to Jerry's earlier reference to his moral superiority to others in society, when he argued: 'Mary, Mary, I am pleading for your love. With Labour, Mary, humanity is above everything; we are the Leaders in the fight for a new life.'

When I once argued aloud that O'Casey is here referring, however obliquely, to betrayal within the Labour movement that he had seen at close hand, a colleague replied, 'But surely you can't expect Devine, just because he's a socialist, to accept fathering another's child'. There doesn't seem to be much that one can say in reply, save that I see this betrayal by Devine (for such I think O'Casey saw it, in an echo of the earlier betrayal of Mary by Bentham) to be the Labour official's betrayal of his social and political principles. He has no business to make universal claims for his own ideals and those of the trade union movement in general unless he can accept Mary, illegitimate child and all. It is only in the wide context of his own humanitarian claims that we (with Mary) can censure him; but what is indisputable is that Mary's repudiation of his moral position is straight-forward and clear-sighted; there is no whinging self-pity here at all, which makes her subsequent whining comment to her mother – 'My poor little child that'll have no father' – the more noticeably out of character. It seems clearly a device to bring forth Juno's statement of principle. Not all stage directors have liked the contrivance. I recall a letter in *The Guardian* newspaper, at the time the British National Theatre was staging *Juno and the Paycock* in Sir Laurence Olivier's production, which complained that Juno's line about two mothers had been omitted. It seemed to me then that Olivier had cut it, not because he disliked Juno's 'sexist' challenge (if such it is), but because he disliked Mary's uncharacteristic descent into bathos – and it is not possible to omit the latter without sacrificing Juno's response as well.

II

Another prevalent idea concerning O'Casey's Dublin trilogy (and I suppose it would also encompass the *Silver Tassie*, written for production at the Abbey immediately after *The Plough and the Stars*) is that these are, primarily, pacifist plays with the women promoting the anti-war message. In the context of his own superb Easter Week play, *The Scythe and the Sunset*, the playwright Denis Johnston has put forward most persuasively what has by now become a common belief regarding O'Casey's alleged 'pacifism'. The preface to this work, entitled 'Up the Rebels!', contains a number of ideas that are, to me, highly dubious.[2] Johnston claims that the very existence of his own play depends upon an essential inadequacy in O'Casey's Easter Week drama:

As far as I am aware, only one other play about 1916 was performed prior to my own, in spite of all impressions to the contrary . . . The other Easter Week play is, of course, Sean O'Casey's finest piece of writing. *The Plough and the Stars* – the play of which the title of mine is an obvious parody . . . Neither in verbiage, plot nor sentiments does this play of mine presume to bear any relation to its magnificent predecessor. The only point in so titling it lies in the fact that *The Plough* is essentially a pacifist play, implying that if only man had 'a titther o' sense', these outbreaks of destruction and bloodshed would never occur. As a quiet man who, nevertheless, is not a pacifist, I cannot accept the fact that, theatrically, Easter Week should remain indefinitely with only an anti-war comment, however fine. So also, it may be noticed that the mouthpiece for most of O'Casey's pacifism is provided by his women; whereas in actual fact the women in Ireland, ever since the Maud Gonne era, have been the most vocal part of its militancy. If

I can claim nothing else, I can at least point with some complacency to the fact that – when it comes to the point – both my women are killers.

Johnston's prose here is deliberately modulated so that the final five-word assertion ('when it comes to the point – *both my women are killers*') comes through in a particularly pointed manner to challenge and shock the reader, especially as the dramatist counterpoints the 'complacency' of his claim with the intentionally shocking word 'killers' applied to his two leading women characters. Elsewhere, in another reference to his Easter Week drama, he goes out of his way to stress the militancy of several of his women figures; it is clear that Johnston wants not only to implicate the women of Ireland in what Yeats called 'the growing murderousness of the world'[3] but to make quite sure that his readers will not in any way overlook feminine complicity in the continuing state of violence in his native land.

Johnston's comments were written long before violence once again erupted in Northern Ireland in the late 1960s, so they cannot be construed as opposing (as now we can see they do) the popular identification in the world's press of women with what became known as the Peace Movement in the North. Of course, as the Peace Movement *did* arise from the efforts of two Ulster women, in conjunction with their many friends and supporters (mostly women, at least to start with), this equation is valid and was bound to arise. It is only just or, at least, even-handed to add, however, that at all times from the beginning of the recent troubles to the present moment women have also been in the forefront of the most militant elements there. I mention this as an historical fact and without, I hope, any of the emotional *frisson* that Johnston wants to accompany his remarks on female aggressiveness. The Civil Rights movement in Northern Ireland in the late 'Sixties and early 'Seventies was assertive, verbally, but did not believe in physical violence to achieve its essentially democratic ends. As its objectives encompassed improving housing and living conditions as well as employment, and reforming electoral redistribution (in the case of gerrymandered electoral registers and unfair geographical boundaries to electoral divisions, both local and national), it is not surprising that women should be intimately concerned with the direction and promotion of the movement, nor that they should be strongly committed and vocally assertive on the streets and at the barricades.

It is understandable, indeed, that in Northern Ireland in recent years, as in the South in earlier times, women have been prominent in the political agitation. In each case musical voices have become strident and some hearts, presumably, have become 'enchanted' to stones which may 'trouble the living stream'. Behind the barricades as in the Peace Movement (which more recently seems to have run out of ideas if not conviction) we may thus find women prominently featured. That seems to have been a recurrent pattern throughout history. If Dervorgilla brought in the foreign invaders, ostensibly to aid one Irish side against another, then public figures like Maud Gonne and the Countess Markiewicz have been equally avid in attempts to repel such intruders. In Irish mythology and throughout Irish history and literature, a martial feminine pattern may be discerned: the Morigu is a fearsome Goddess of War, Maeve (especially) and Emer are dominant fighting figures (among many others) in early sagas as in later retellings, and the pirate Grace or Grainne O'Malley in the reign of Queen Elizabeth I was as redoubtable a warrior as was Queen Boadicea or, for that matter, Elizabeth herself.

Does this mean that O'Casey's realisation of Irish womanhood is either false or, at least, incomplete? Not at all. It means that Denis Johnston, like many critics before and since, has misinterpreted O'Casey's plays, including the one that is the focus of his criticism. *The Plough and the Stars* is full of references to militant women and shows us several of them in action. Nora Clitheroe, it is true, does seem to embody a pacifist strain projected onto a level beyond that of the individual alone. At one point, distracted to frenzy and grief by her husband's participation in the street fighting, she says: 'An' there's no woman gives a son or a husband to be killed – if they say it, they're lyin', lyin', against God, Nature, an' against themselves!' In her pregnant state she obviously speaks for the forces that make for life. That she is meant to have this larger significance is borne out by a statement made by her creator during the press controversy that swirled about the play at the time of its initial production in Dublin. In a letter to the *Irish Times* for 19 February 1926 (reprinted in the *Irish Independent* the following day) O'Casey asserted: 'Nora voices not only the feeling of Ireland's womanhood, but also the women of the human race. The safety of her brood is the true morality of every woman. A mother does not like her son to be killed – she does not like him even to get married.' Yet this very viewpoint was disputed by a group of Republican women, whose aggressive opposition led to riots in the Abbey Theatre as well as giving rise to heated disputes in many Irish newspapers and journals. Nora, in the play itself, tells of similar violence by women during the Rising: 'One blasted hussy at a barricade told me to go home an' not be tryin' to dishearten th' men . . . That I wasn't worthy to bear a son to a man that was out fightin' for freedom . . . I clawed at her, an' smashed her in th' face till we were separated.' No passive or submissive woman herself, she can be equally aggressive in her struggle against what she conceives to be a foolish and inopportune act of political madness.

Nora's is the only feminine voice raised in opposition to the armed conflict in the course of *The Plough and the Stars*. Bessie Burgess is, of course, vehemently hostile to the revolution – but that is because, as a Protestant loyalist, she upholds the *status quo*; moreover, with a son fighting in France with the British army, she vigorously supports the larger war effort in Europe. On the other hand, Jinnie Gogan clearly sides with the revolutionaries ('Oh, they're not cowards anyway', she contradicts Nora) and shouts slogans about 'poor little Catholic Ireland' in answer to Bessie's trumpeting of official British propaganda on behalf of 'poor little Catholic Belgium'. In this scene in Act II, as in several others throughout the play, the two women actually come to blows (in Act I it is Bessie and Nora who quarrel); and there are a number of fights in which women are actively engaged, physically or verbally, including Jack Clitheroe's altercation with Bessie in Act I and the latter's constant verbal sniping at everyone else in the tenement during Act III. On one level, *The Plough* can be envisaged as a series of brilliantly orchestrated quarrels, during which brawling becomes virtually an art form in itself – and one in which the female figures more than hold their own. Certainly, in this context, there is no way in which women can be seen as less aggressive than men; the militancy of a Grainne O'Malley, a Maud Gonne or Countess Markiewicz is thus concretely embodied in O'Casey's drama, and in no more shocking a visual image than in his strongest anti-war play, *The Silver Tassie*. When the curtain rises on the first act we are shown an attractive young Dublin girl polishing a Lee-Enfield rifle with devout care. In her devotion to the war hero, Harry Heegan, Susie Monican is only too representative of a hero-worship that extends to everyone we encounter in slum society in the play. Chanting evangelically in favour of the British war effort during the first World War, Susie represents visually and verbally a fervent priestess serving before the shrine to a young athlete who equally clearly stands for brute force and aggressively competitive drive. The tenement women in this play are, without exception, glad to get their menfolk onto the troopship taking them back to active service in France; all have a vested interest (either to preserve a government grant or to have a good time without a husband's interference) in seeing the soldiers back in uniform after leave at home. The result is savage satire of materialistic selfishness and war-worship on a shockingly large scale. It is impossible to believe that 'the mouthpiece for most of O'Casey's pacifism is provided by his women', here or elsewhere, as Denis Johnston claims. While the total thematic emphasis in these early works is certainly antagonistic to violence and bloodshed, the role of the women is undoubtedly far more complex and contradictory than Johnston suggests.

III

When we come down to it, the truest and the most telling artistic testimony to O'Casey's understanding of women is almost certainly to be found in the short story section in his 1934 grab-bag of literary odds and ends entitled *Windfalls*. The four stories that appeared in this book were reprinted in *The Green Crow* in the mid-1950s. All four are strongly sympathetic to the women who are realised in the action of each tale, and three of the four are narrated from the woman's point of view. It seems worth looking at them here, therefore, especially as they are usually overlooked in evaluations of O'Casey's writings.

The first of these stories was written in 1925; the other three in 1928. The earliest one is concerned with the thoughts and feelings of a teenage girl, dying of tuberculosis in a Dublin tenement. Her name is Mollser: indeed, the story when originally published in the *Irish Statesman* in April 1925 was entitled 'Mollser'; later it was re-titled 'A Fall in a Gentle Wind'. Unlike the consumptive child with the same name who dies in the tenement in the course of *The Plough and the Stars*, Mollser is taken away from the tenement at the end of the story to await her end in a Hospice for the Dying. A similar incident is recounted in the playwright's fourth book of autobiography, *Inishfallen, Fare Thee Well*. There, the painful incident is related with sympathetic concern for the child and her parents (who, as in the story, are unable to look after the girl properly in the final stages of the disease), but it is not narrated from the doomed girl's point of view. Instead, her unwilling committal to the care of the nuns at the Hospice and her departure from the tenement on a stretcher are described through O'Casey's own eyes, helped by the words of the girl's father, a tenement friend of the author. The short story, however, is told entirely from Mollser's viewpoint; it takes place – to start with – on a fine day in late spring, only to flash forward to the summer when her condition has worsened though she still desperately believes that each new day will see her take a turn for the better. 'A Fall in a Gentle Wind' is an appropriate title for a simple story characterised by its quiet compassion for the young girl, 'pallid with the mournful delicacy of disease', and for all life worn out and wasted before its due time. In

the tenement opposite hers, we hear, there is another representative victim of slum poverty in 'the coiled-up frame of little Alice Tait
. . . gripped in the Laocoön vice of creeping paralysis'.

The author's sympathies extend beyond the struggling human
flotsam and jetsam of the slums to encompass even the stunted trees
there. Of the heroine of the story, for instance, it is said:

A vague sense of kinship moved her to sympathy as she looked at the frail,
thin trunk, like her own shrinking body; the fragile branches stretching
towards the sky as if appealing for deliverance; the leaves murmuring a
gentle protest, and the whole nature of the little captive from the wood,
pregnant with bewilderment at the loss of its heritage of solitude . . . A
half-hidden gleam of subconscious envy faintly glimmered from the brown,
wistful eyes of Mollser as she watched the animated excitement of the little
leaves sharing in the motions of the sparrows springing with an exultant
celerity from spray to spray; she gently thrilled as she noticed the rapid
pulsing movement of their little throats, chirrruping with the recklessness of
elemental vigour, their tiny, diamond-like eyes, luminous with the confi-
dent hilarity of a natural discipline that gave them the fullness of life.
And Mollser shivered as she vaguely thought that life was more abundant
in a common sparrow than it was in her: song and rhythm and motion,
against weakness, disease, and death, a fragile feathered morsel of life, that
even her little, wasted hand could clutch and banish from the universe,
vibrant with the vigour that her body . . . would never know.

The concern and empathy is strongly in evidence, though the writing is at times somewhat immature, as it is in that extract.

The other three stories are more accomplished pieces of writing.
'I Wanna Woman' is a lively realistic satire of a self-centred sensual-
ist, who, having temporarily satisfied his desires with the services of
an intelligent and sensitive prostitute, exhibits his 'morning after'
guilt feelings in a horrifying self-righteous and puritanical vicious-
ness. The young whore, by contrast, comes out of the encounter
with some credit but she is not central to the narrative. The remaining two tales are much more apposite for my purposes. 'The Job'
realises, through its young female protagonist's thoughts and feelings, the woman, once again, as victim of the social system. Here the
unnamed heroine is a girl on the fringe of the entertainment industry, auditioning for a place in a chorus line and having to endure the
usual occupational hazard: sexual harassment from theatre mana-
gers and producers. The heroine here, like the leading lady of
Within the Gates (a play being written at the same time), is a
sensitive and fastidious woman who, awkward and ill at ease, finds
such harassment very difficult to handle. Hard up, financially, and
anxious for employment, she endures the preliminary lascivious

attentions of a promoter, following a job interview, and cannot find it in her to stand out against his insistent invitations to a quiet supper one evening later in the week. Subsequently, in an interior monologue she examines her incapacity, makes resolutions for the future that we cannot help thinking are unduly optimistic, and ends up criticising her own social incompetence:

It was something to be breathing the air even of Piccadilly again after that sombre, stuffy, sinister-looking torture-chamber of an office . . . Wanted a lot for four pounds a week . . . Little enough for work that sweated her for hours every night without having to let herself be mauled about into the bargain. She wished she was a little better at that kind of game. She could make quite a lot out of it if she wasn't so damned shy. Somehow or other she couldn't make use of it as other girls did. No good at a business deal. She'd try this time, anyhow; everyone had to learn, and after a little practice she'd get going all right. How to start, that was the difficulty . . . She might hint that she owed some rent. No, that would be too common. She'd have to find a fairer way than that . . . One thing, she'd have to hold him off for a time, job or no job. A woman shrinks in the mind of a man when he swings her easily into his arms. She was sorry now she'd accepted his offer to supper on Wednesday. Should she put him off a little longer? Wednesday? Oh, no, couldn't: sorry; full up the whole week. Something on every night. Every night? Every night, my dear man; sorry. Next week, maybe; ring me up some evening and we'll see. Instead of that she hesitated, stammered, and gave him Wednesday. How is it she couldn't do these things properly, like other girls? Some kink in her somewhere.

In the reference to her possession of scruples and lack of brazen insincerity as a 'kink', we see the triumph of cynical materialism. Everyone else in her society (including the other girls in her position) seems to accept the system; she therefore feels it must be she herself who is at fault, with 'some kink in her somewhere'.

Her thoughts turn to her steady boyfriend, who seems (by her own account) genuinely fond of her. It is the ironies of her position which are uppermost in her mind, however, as she reflects:

If she went with Jim tonight, she'd have to be careful not to let him go too far. Oh, dear, she had to be careful of everyone. Careful of Jim because he was too poor; and careful of this old buffer because he was too rich. Careful of Jim because she wanted to give herself to him, and careful of the other because she didn't want to give herself to him. It was a curious world . . . It was easier to put Jim off than this one. Jim was young and poor, and could wait; this one was impatient and rich, and she wanted the job.

The story opened with the girl's looking forward to a pre-arranged dance with Jim that very evening; it ends with her receiving a telegram from him changing the date to the following Wednesday –

the evening now 'booked' by her prospective new employer.

O'Casey's finest story is undoubtedly the one entitled 'The Star Jazzer', a tender evocation of a tenement housewife's unexpressed (and, for her, inexpressible) desire for a finer way of life, amid the squalid mental and physical drudgery which comprises virtually her entire existence. Again, the heroine is an anonymous figure but her personal and her social situations eventually become explicit through the stream of her consciousness that surges through the story. A young mother of six living children (and one dead), she lives ten flights up a tall 'filth-fostered' house sheltering ten families and a total population of forty-five people. Her family of eight occupies a one-room apartment, with two younger children sharing the conjugal bed. The story itself is something of a short-lived epiphany in a life that now has few moments of heightened experience or revelation of any sort. It realises a brief spot of time at the end of a typical hard washing-day. She had kept going all day long from six in the morning until midnight, when, for the last time in a day that has seen her descend and ascend two hundred tall flights of stairs, she makes her final trip to the communal water tap outside the house in the tenement yard. Everyone else in the crowded building appears to have gone to bed. A large glittering star directly above her head gradually takes over her only half-awake mind until she is momentarily obsessed and partially mesmerised by it. Her sensitised awareness of the star's beauty, and her wish both to worship and to re-create that beauty in her dance to the apparent motion of the star, to assert her human worth and defy the harsh conditions of her environment, are unconscious or but partially conscious elements that are realised realistically in the story while yet, at the same time, the experience possesses a symbolic quality that might be called, in the best sense of the term, Lawrentian. In *Sons and Lovers*, for instance, Paul Morel's mother, locked out of her house by her drunken husband, experiences what one can only describe as a kind of mystical experience in the gradually hypnotic moonlight; a comparable moment of truth occurs during the concluding night scene in Albert Camus's story 'The Adulterous Woman' in his collection *Exile and the Kingdom*. In each case the woman's temporary release from an emotionally as well as physically oppressive life is realised in heightened sensuous prose that nonetheless never soars out of sight beyond the immediate restrictions of her earthly 'prison'. In 'The Star-Jazzer', for instance, it is said of the heroine:

She felt a surge moving through her body. A desire to circle around the lonely yard, surrounded by the surly-featured tenements, now dark and still, sheltering the sleeping, to sing softly, to move and wag her body through the rhythms of a Charleston or a Jazz; to show the star that, in spite of seven kids carried in ten years, her figure was still shapely; that her hair was still long and thick, and the gold gleams in the brown weren't all gone; that her face, hiding its lines in the darkness, had all its beauty left. She bent back her head and stared up at the star. Then she began to move her body to the tune and motions of a Jazz, circling round the yard while the water poured lazily from the pipe, filled the pail, and flowed over the rim, down the sides, and disappeared into the gully beneath. She stepped forward with her left foot, then with her right, brought her feet together and dipped by bending her legs backward from the knees. She moved forward, twisted, turned and came back again. Step, step, step, together, dip, with her head bent back, gazing at the star. As she moved she felt her wet skirt sopping, sopping against her knees, so as she moved on, step, step, she unloosened her skirt at the waist, together, dip; and as she rose to step forward again, the skirt fell from her, and she danced on in her short black petticoat. With her hair flowing down, in her untidily buttoned blouse, dingy black petticoat, patched shoes, and imitation silk stockings, ribbed and scarred with many a mended ladder, round the tenement-enclosed yard she turned, bent, circled, advanced, retreated, across and around the yard, singing with her head bent back, staring at the star.

Here, we experience something of the proud movement of the anonymous heroine's celebration of life, joy and beauty; it is but a short-lived epiphany, however, for the soul-sapping drudgery that is the substance of her daily life overcomes her by the close of this story. Even as the exhausted woman submits to her husband's loveless embraces, in a bed shared with two restless children, she can still see 'the star that had seen her dancing gleaming grandly down at her through the window of the skylight'.

In their aspirations, as much as in their actions, the young women in O'Casey's work embody hope for the future. Their desire for greater fulfilment in life than is at present attainable by them is, by its very nature and by their ignorance, inadequately expressed and is not even wholly understood by them. In many ways it is similar to the inarticulate longing of the women in D.H. Lawrence's *The Rainbow*, where there is, likewise, a cleavage in sensibility and awareness between them and the men. In the beginning of the novel the men in the farming community are content with their hard-working lives, in physical harmony with the soil. The womenfolk, however, are dissatisfied: they 'wanted another form of life than this'. The woman craved to achieve a 'higher being', as Lawrence wrote, 'if not in herself, then in her children', and she thus sought to 'learn the entry into the finer, more vivid circle of life'. Lawrence's novel concretely realises this yearning ambition in the women, and the clash in the Brangwen family between the sexes which is one of the results of the women's quest. A similar conflict is found in O'Casey's plays, though presented by the playwright in less overt terms. Even so, we see in the actions of Minnie Powell, Mary Boyle, Nora Clitheroe, Lorna Marthraun and many other women characters faltering attempts to find an 'entry into the finer, more vivid circle of life', and in Juno Boyle and in Nora the conviction 'to achieve this higher being', if not in themselves, then in their children. To make this claim is not to deny that Nora and Juno are themselves criticised in the course of their respective plays.

Their sensitivity and vision are, understandably, restricted by circumstances and environment, and O'Casey makes the limitations quite apparent, as indeed does D.H. Lawrence with the women in his novel. For both writers, however, the important quality is the women's awareness of finer things beyond their immediate experience; and their aspiration to achieve them or to see that their children do so.

The heroine of Olive Schreiner's novel *The Story of an African Farm* exclaims bitterly at one point: 'There was never a man who said one word for woman but he said two for man, and three for the whole human race.' Within its context of time and place (the South African karoo towards the end of the nineteenth century) the statement is hardly an exaggeration and, even within a larger world today, it still remains a far from irrelevant touchstone. The plays and prose writings of Sean O'Casey do exhibit the presence of one of several honourable exceptions this century: for, if his later writings (unlike the earlier ones) show him capable of uttering at least one word for man, he was throughout a long life always prepared to speak two for woman. Often, indeed, two were the minimum he would offer, spoken frequently and consistently in a tone of urgent compassion and understanding.

NOTES

1 Jack Mitchell is a no-nonsense critic with some refreshing as well as some wayward views on the women characters in O'Casey's plays. He is particularly concerned to question whether or not the women in the early Dublin plays are heroic; his own evaluation is infused (and I think confused also) by Marxist ideology and a hatred for Christianity. Regarding Minnie Powell in *The Shadow of a Gunman*, Mitchell quotes Robert Hogan's view that 'The theme of the play concerns the difference between true and false bravery. The characters who are truly brave – Maguire, Minnie, Mrs. Henderson – are not talkers, but doers', and goes on to say: 'In talking of women characters like Minnie and Juno (*Juno and the Paycock*) David Krause pronounces the women to possess "the only kind of untainted heroism that O'Casey recognizes". This has become something of an "established truth" in conventional O'Casey criticism. Nevertheless, it is not true. As regards Minnie – bravery functioning in the context sketched in above

is functioning falsely and is therefore not true concrete bravery. For the same reason she cannot function as heroic alternative to the pseudo-heroic figures. Minnie is herself conceived by the dramatist as part of his systematic exposure of empty heroism and his puncturing of out-of-date and deadly heroic myths. As things are, Minnie is still only the shadow of a hero. In this way the very qualities of courage and devotion which ought to be helping the people to emancipate themselves are made to function in the opposite direction, against the people, as factors contributing to their own destruction. The women suffer to an important extent from the same basic "disease" as the men. Minnie eggs Davoren on along the line that leads to disaster. In this sense she is his "accomplice." ' (J. Mitchell, *The Essential O'Casey* [New York, 1980], p. 28). And, of *Juno and the Paycock*, the same critic writes (while discussing the necessity for 'heroes of a new type' in the ideological struggle in Ireland): 'But is Juno not a heroine? The mother-cult has played a big part in Irish consciousness from the Virgin Mary to Mother Machree waiting for her sons and daughters to return from exile, and Juno too, is named after the Mother of Gods (what Gods!). Does O'Casey the myth-breaker make an exception here and add his mite to the myth? Many critics have thought so. Krause says she has "the heroic stature of her namesake". Cowasjee agrees: "Juno, the greatest of O'Casey's heroines, has often been referred to as the greatest mother in drama. In the midst of shirkers, braggarts, the wrong-principled and the good-for-nothings, she alone shows courage and common sense." In the opinion of the Soviet critic Sarukhanyan, however, "O'Casey does not idealise his heroine", but sees her as a calculated rebuff to the glorified figure of Kathleen ni Houlihan as symbolic of Ireland' (pp. 54–55). Mitchell admits that it 'would be foolish to deny that there is a kind of heroism in Juno', praises her as 'the master myth-destroyer and puncturer of puffed-up peacockery', but then spends a good deal of time trying to cut her down to less heroic size. His final assessment is that 'Juno is no "positive hero" shining among the human dross. To an important degree her characterisation is part of the general process of hero-breaking . . . There is as little justification here as there was in the case of *The Gunman* for maintaining that O'Casey glorifies the women characters as against the men.' (p. 58).

There is no point in here contesting these assertions (the paper does so by implication), but it might be useful to quote O'Casey himself on the bravery of women. The following extract from a telephone conversation between Don Ross and the playwright was printed in the *New York Herald Tribune* for 16 November 1958:

Ross: I want to get back to *The Shadow of a Gunman* for a moment. I've heard it said that in your plays it's the women who turn out to be the courageous ones.

O'Casey: Women must be more courageous than the men. Courage doesn't consist in just firing a pistol and killing somebody, or taking the risk of another firing a pistol and killing you. I wouldn't call that courage at all, I'd call it stuipidity.

Ross: What does a woman's courage consist in?

O'Casey: Fortitude – and patience – and understanding.

Ross: Is this true, then, that you think that women are more courage-ous than men?

O'Casey: In life, yes. They're much more near to the earth than men are. Men are more idealistic, stupidly idealistic. They're not as realistic as women. The woman has to be nearer the earth than the man.

2   In a preface to this play, entitled 'Up the Rebels!', Johnston laments that *'The*

Scythe and the Sunset shows every sign of turning out to be one of those elusive phenomena – a play without a public'; to which one can only retort that this fact is most regrettable and, it is to be hoped, will be remedied at some early date by increased public exhibition until the play gains the critical recognition that its dramatic merit undoubtedly deserves. Caustic wit and a strongly dialectical technique have not prevented Bernard Shaw's plays from popular acceptance on stage, including the stage in Ireland; why should not Johnston's essentially Shavian drama itself achieve similar success in his native land – and elsewhere, too?

3   W.B. Yeats, *Autobiographies* (London, 1966), p. 192.

THE LOOK OF A QUEEN

HUGH KENNER

In the spring of 1977 I was preparing the script for a one-hour radio programme devoted to James Joyce: an instalment of National Public Radio's *A Question of Place*. Since ours was to be a pilot for the series, i.e. a showpiece to attract Foundation money, the producer had decided that we should be wise to spare no reasonable expense. For the sake of real Irish voices we would do most of our recording in Dublin, and I decided to devote much of our air-time to dramatizations of key Joycean scenes, enacted by Irish actors.

This would not entail any of the slick rewriting that dramatization of fiction normally requires. One of my first discoveries had been that Joyce wrote every line of dialogue exactly as someone in Dublin might speak it. The way his people talk is not shaped by the conventions of fiction, the way fictional dialogue is shaped in Dickens or in Henry James. It is shaped by his exact ear and by the conventions of some ideal stage, more realistic even than Ibsen's. And his scenes, as I soon found out, are in general completely realized, all the spoken lines written, none subsumed into novelist's paraphrase. So much is this his norm that when, as in the bedroom dialogue between Leopold Bloom and Molly early in *Ulysses*, speeches are missing, hence things left unsaid, we are meant to notice something about the way these two communicate, with gaps and expressive silences.

Joyce, it seemed, had meant what he had Stephen Dedalus say about an evolving hierarchy of literary genres, Lyric, Epic, Dramatic, with drama at the summit. Though his one play is his least successful work, his art was the dramatist's.

Moreover, Stephen Dedalus, who is no more scrupulous than W.B. Yeats about citing his sources and his points of departure, seems to have been revising a sequence that Yeats enunciated in 1893. Yeats claimed that the genres had evolved in a different order, Epic, Drama, Lyric: Homer, Aeschylus, the Greek Anthology: the subjective lyric therefore (in which Yeats excelled) a consummation. Though Yeats was already contemplating the Irish National Theatre, he seemed not really to believe in the stage: not

115

even in his much later ventures into symbolic drama did he wholly give over the idea that drama was a means to an end, the raising of national consciousness, what Stephen calls a kinetic and therefore impure art.

Among the last glimpses we have of Joyce in Dublin is Joseph Holloway's mention of his visit, on 10 June 1904, to a rehearsal of two plays of Synge's. In the theatre, and notably at the side of Synge whom he had met in Paris two years previously: such, insofar as he had one, seems to have been James Joyce's elected public Dublin context.

So Joyce had done all the real work, and my chief task would be devising continuity for the programme. For any scene that I chose to mount, the spoken words were waiting on his page for me to transcribe. I had only to omit the narrative bridges as I typed out scripts for my actors. An eager novice at the radio game, I soon had a sheaf of typescript for my producer, Robert Montiegel.

Montiegel, weighing things I had paid no heed to, notably the budget, was quick to count up the number of speaking parts. They totalled something like thirty-eight: so much for my innocence. Clearly it was out of the question to pay that many actors, let alone cope with such a traffic jam in the studio. The parts would need distributing among a smaller number, and it was up to me to indicate how they could be doubled and tripled.

That was when I made my next fundamental discovery: Joyce himself thought in terms of doubled parts. That people play roles analogous to the roles of others, that Tom Kernan the tea-taster doubles with Leopold Bloom, that sundry antagonists of Stephen's resemble either his father or Buck Mulligan, this was not a structural conceit peculiar to *Ulysses*, but omnipresent in *Dubliners* and the *Portrait* as well, and central moreover to the conception *Finnegans Wake* exfoliates, that any family is a repertory company. Six men and two women, I quickly discovered, could play every part in every scene I had chosen, especially for an audience that would not be able to see them. No more than any other fictional ensemble is the James Joyce Repertory Company visible. Appearance matters little; voices matter greatly, and the roles implied by voices. And Joyce uses a finite, small inventory of roles. Six men, give or take a couple: say five to seven. But, trial repeatedly proved, exactly two women. *That* was interesting.

The Irish Literary Revival, it grows commonplace to observe, was pre-eminently an affair of the theatre, and James Joyce in his student days was around for its beginnings. On 8 May 1899, in the spring of his freshman year, he attended at the Antient Concert Rooms on Brunswick Street the inauguration of the National Theatre, when

English actors did what they could with *The Countess Cathleen*
while stage doors creaked and tin-tray thunder rattled, and he made
a point of not signing a student manifesto against it. *A Portrait of the
Artist as a Young Man* recalls the affair without signs of enthusiasm:

He was alone at the side of the balcony, looking out of jaded eyes at the
culture of Dublin in the stalls and at the tawdry scenecloths and human dolls
framed by the garish lamps of the stage. A burly policeman sweated behind
him and seemed at every moment about to act. The catcalls and hisses and
mocking cries ran in rude gusts round the hall from his scattered fellow
students.

> – A libel on Ireland!
> – Made in Germany!
> – Blasphemy!
> – We never sold our faith!
> – No Irish woman ever did it!
> – We want no amateur atheists.
> – We want no budding buddhists.

Here the word 'act' is used only of the policeman; the actors are
'human dolls', the scenecloths 'tawdry'. It was not the play, it was
the verse of Yeats the lyricist that seized hold of Joyce's memory,
these farewell words for instance of the Countess:

> *Bend. down your faces, Oona and Aleel,*
> *I gaze upon them as the swallow gazes*
> *Upon the nest under the eave before*
> *He wander the wide waters.*

. . . A soft liquid joy flowed through the words where the soft long vowels
hurtled noiselessly and fell away, lapping and flowing back and ever shaking
the white bells of their waves in mute chime and mute peal and low soft
swooning cry . . . [pp. 225–6].

By 1902, though, Yeats had managed something much more like
a play: *Cathleen ni Houlihan*, with Maud Gonne in the title role
keening the words that in fourteen years would speed patriots to
death – 'If any one would give me help he must give me himself, he
must give me all'.

> (Did that play of mine send out
> Certain men the English shot?

was a question to torment Yeats decades later.) And there was a
stirring exchange at the close:

– Did you see an old woman going down the path?
– I did not, but I saw a young girl, and she had the walk of a queen.

It was maybe in brooding over that metamorphosis that Joyce evolved his own doubled woman, the reason we need two actresses. Thirty years later, as he toiled on *Finnegans Wake*, those words of Yeats were still ringing in his head:

A space. Who are you? The cat's mother. A time. What do you lack? The look of a queen [FW223]. . . .

The look of a queen, that is what Joyce rejects. He sees the old woman who beckons to young men to go off and die, and not marry, and he will let no fine talk deflect attention from that.

It was in the summer of 1904, in a story the first version of which appeared in AE's *Irish Homestead*, that James Joyce arranged his own first iconic tableau: a household consisting of a deranged old paralysed celibate and two women. In the narrative forefront is a puzzled boy who is interested in the old man, once a priest, now dead. But the story is not called 'The Father', it is called 'The Sisters', and the sisters are exhibited with grim thoroughness. Their names are Nannie Flynn and Eliza Flynn, and they run the household now and control the memories. Nannie from the beginning to the end of the story says nothing whatsoever. She exhibits the corpse, she prays, she pours sherry, she falls asleep. Eliza does none of these things; she does nothing whatever save talk. Joyce seems to have derived them from the scriptural sisters of Bethany: Martha who troubled herself about many things; and Mary who had chosen the better part, which was exchanging words with the Lord.

In Dublin after nineteen centuries Martha and Mary are subdued and crazed. The busy sister will do nothing but show and pray and pour only because the wits to speak are no longer left her. The talkative sister prates of carriages with 'rheumatic wheels' and misses the import of whatever she narrates, such as the occasion when their brother was found sitting in the dark in his confession-box, 'wide-awake and laughing-like softly to himself'. It is not thinkable to her that he may have lost his faith; he was simply 'too scrupulous always'.

Martha and Mary had a brother, Lazarus, whom Jesus restored to life. Nannie and Eliza had a brother, James, who lies upstairs dead now ('No one would think he'd make such a beautiful corpse') and only comes momentarily back to life in the young boy's fevered imagination. When he was alive 'You wouldn't hear him in the house any more than now', and now – this is just after Eliza has told about the laughing –

She stopped suddenly as if to listen. I too listened; but there was no sound in the house . . . .

The same as when he was alive: it is a dubious resurrection.

This story, with the unheard laughter at its ending, is our first glimpse of Joyce's systematic doubling of female parts. The next story he wrote was 'Eveline', about a woman who will spend the rest of her life torn in two, between the family duties she assumed as a promise to her dying mother, and her fantasies of what she may have missed by not going off with 'Frank'. Here Joyce is especially subtle in allowing us to perceive Frank as likely a skilled seducer whom Eveline was too inexperienced to suspect.

We next come upon Polly Mooney and her mother. 'Mrs Mooney was a butcher's daughter. She was a woman who was quite able to keep things to herself: a determined woman.' Her estranged husband has become 'a shabby stooped little drunkard with a white face'. Polly on the other hand is 'very lively', and 'The intention' – this is worded with fine impersonality – 'The intention was to give her the run of the young men' in Mrs Mooney's boarding house. She glances upward when she speaks, 'like a little perverse madonna', and between her and her mother there exists an intricate unworded understanding. So she seduces Bob Doran, knowing (Joyce does not put it so bluntly) that her mother means her to. She is 19, he 35. Mrs Mooney 'thought of some mothers she knew who could not get their daughters off their hands'. It is a simple matter – one confrontation merely – for her to ensure that marriage will follow the seduction. While this unpleasantness is taking its course Polly lies upstairs, lost in intricate hopes and visions, until at the sound of her mother's voice 'she remembered what she had been waiting for'. They are a symbiotic pair, these two, one woman divided between two generations. Together they are a man-trap.

In the story called 'A Mother' Mrs Kearney and her daughter Kathleen make a similar pair, except that Kathleen is steered not towards a wedded future but towards *no* future. The context of 'A Mother' is the Revival:

When the Irish Revival began to be appreciable Mrs Kearney determined to take advantage of her daughter's name and brought an Irish teacher to the house. Kathleen and her sister sent Irish picture postcards to their friends and these friends sent back other Irish picture postcards . . . .

Not only does she think to exploit the fact that her daughter's name is Kathleen, she is to be found brokering with a Mr Holohan for Kathleen's musical services, and pulls Kathleen out when the money is insufficient. Wracked between Kathleen Kearney and Mr Holohan, who has overestimated the appeal of patriotic concerts, Kathleen ni Houlihan is divided indeed.

In 'The Dead', finally, these doublings are redoubled. As in 'The Sisters', we have a gaunt house containing two old women, Aunt Kate and Aunt Julia. As in 'The Boarding House' and 'A Mother', we find two generations of women under one roof: the old women's niece Mary Jane seems to have little future save in teaching music as her aunts had done. Gretta Conroy, the wife of the old women's nephew, is polarized in her husband's mind against an aggressively patriotic young woman named Miss Ivors. (She existed, by the way; her name was Kathleen Sheehy; after she married she had a son named Conor Cruise O'Brien.) And like the girl in 'Eveline', Gretta by the end of the story is divided in herself: between her living husband with his pince-nez and his goloshes and a lost romantic vision in which a young man named Michael stood for love of her in the rain 'at the end of the wall where there was a tree'. Cradling the romance she remembers from her girlhood in Galway far in the west, she ruins Gabriel's evening.

Yes, Michael Furey is dead. Gabriel seeks to prolong their talk. He asks,

– And what he die of so young, Gretta? Consumption, was it?
– I think he died for me, she answered.
A vague terror seized Gabriel at this answer. . . .

– as well it might have, since Gretta has inadvertantly quoted from the play which Joyce thought lay on the Irish imagination like frost: from *Cathleen ni Houlihan*. The following dialogue from the play is also about a death in Galway:

Michael. What is it that you are singing, ma'am?
Old Woman. Singing I am about a man I knew one time, yellow-haired Donagh that was hanged in Galway. . . .
Michael. What was it brought him to his death?
Old Woman. He died for love of me: many a man has died for love of me.

'I think he died for me': Gretta Conroy does not know that she has echoed the words of sinister old Cathleen, nor does she confront the sad thrill she receives from supposing she has perhaps caused someone's death. Is that not a woman's romantic prerogative?
Gretta's luck runs to men with the names of archangels: Michael,

Gabriel. A suburban 'lure of the fallen seraphim' (p. 217), she has terminated the happiness and the life of poor Michael and is now ruining more than an amorous evening for her husband Gabriel. Something is dying inside Gabriel, not to be revived. He has entered the nightmare of history, where the definition of love is not wishing to live.

He thought of how she who lay beside him had locked in her heart for so many years that image of her lover's eyes when he told her that he did not wish to live.

   Generous tears filled Gabriel's eyes. He had never felt like that himself towards any woman but he knew that such a feeling must be love (D 223).

And,

He stretched himself cautiously along under the sheets and lay down beside his wife. One by one they were all becoming shades.

   That the marriage bed has become a bed of death is a theme unmarried Stephen broods on in *Ulysses*: 'Bridebed, childbed, bed of death, ghostcandled'. Stephen too is haunted by a dead woman who is his Cathleen ni Houlihan and demands not less than all. When she was dying she demanded his prayers. He did not pray, but played the song of Fergus to her, the song he had first heard in 1899 at the play about the death of the Countess Cathleen.

> Who will go drive with Fergus now,
> And pierce the deep woods' woven shade,
> And dance upon the level shore? . . .
>
> For Fergus rules the brazen cars. . . .

Reciting this, he celebrates an *aesthetic* god, one who presides over a Yeatsian eternity of dancing (among his mother's faded souvenirs were 'old feathered fans, tasselled dancecards'). Still, her shade will not be placated and her similars are everywhere. She reappears innocuously as the old woman with the milk ('I'm ashamed I don't speak the language myself. I'm told it's a grand language by them that knows'), less casually as Stephen's Italian mistress, the Church ('A crazy queen, old and jealous. Kneel down before me'). And she comes back into his mind from the dead, more than once and notably when he is wantoning amid the lusts of the flesh and she rises through the floor to speak to him of death. ('All must go through it, Stephen. More women than men in the world. You too. Time will come.')

Here we are back with another Yeatsian situation, that of Bridget Bruin in *The Land of Heart's Desire* who pulls her child one way while faeries pull the other and the child dies onstage. Always, for Stephen, women's claims pull deathward: even his sister Dilly, he thinks, pulls him down into 'drowning'.

Molly Bloom's marriage-bed too is notoriously troubled. One kind of split that afflicts her is enacted by the fact that her daughter's name is Milly ('Molly, Milly,' thinks Leopold; 'Same thing watered down') and that she suspects her husband's affections of straying toward Milly, whom she has accordingly sent away. (From the place of exile, darkest Mullingar, Milly fulfils the pattern; she has sent her mother a mere card but her father a letter.) Next, Molly's pending infidelity encourages her husband to double her with the other woman he thinks he might have married, Josie Powell that was, now Mrs Denis Breen. (In the 'Circe' fantasies Molly and Josie alternate but never meet.) Bloom's phantom correspondent, 'Martha Clifford', someone who in 1904 has access to a typewriter, doubles with the only woman we are shown at a typewriter: Miss Dunne, the typist employed by Blazes Boylan, Molly's flame. And the book Miss Dunne is reading has a heroine named 'Marion', which is Molly's real name. . . . On an on, distorted reflections. 'Mocking mirrors' was a phrase Joyce planted early in *Ulysses*. His book's women, doubling, redoubling, mirror one another and mock the reader indeed.

In *Finnegans Wake* the feminine doublings continue. The mother splits into Kate the Scrubwoman and Anna the Allmerciful; the daughter before her mirror splits into two girls or more and makes disorienting talk. For the daughter's talk, Adaline Glasheen showed many years ago, Joyce drew on studies of dissociated personality by the American psychiatrist Morton Prince. For the mother, he drew on his standing inventory of divided heroines, Gretta Conroy, May Dedalus, the unsurnamed Bertha of *Exiles*, Gerty MacDowell, Molly Bloom; on, as everyone knows, myth and music-hall song; on stage-Irishwomen in profusion; on Cathleen ni Houlihan in particular; and on one of the firmest structural conventions of his own work, which always accords the last turn to the feminine will.

It is Gretta who stage-manages the bedroom scene at the end of 'The Dead' by choosing to lie with a ghost; it is Bertha who dictates the end of *Exiles* when she accuses a man who is present in body of being absent in spirit: 'O my strange wild lover, come back to me again' (against which set Pegeen Mike's 'O my grief, I've lost him surely. I've lost the only Playboy of the Western World'). It is Molly Bloom who fills a marital vacuum by reliving 'the day I got him to propose to me', in words that impede our disentangling her suitor, now husband, Leopold on Howth from the object of her first passion, Lieutenant Mulvey on Gibraltar: the Poldy she sees every day, and Mulvey whom she didn't see again after a wild moment twenty years ago.

So now at the end of the last book, Anna, not awake, addresses a man who, structural analogy persuades us, must be thought of as in some sense absent.

And here, where there is no consensus, we must make certain postulations. Joyce once spoke of the way in which he had chosen to tell 'the story of this Chapelizod family', and however uncertain its outlines we may feel sure that beneath the murky waters of the *Wake* a family has been engulfed, a small cluster of living people of whose doings and fortunes Joyce was sure. Though 'the unfacts, did we possess them, are too imprecisely few to warrant our certitude' (FW 57), we may hazard a few guesses. There has been a wake, therefore a death, seemingly having had to do with guilt and a scaffold. The time is after the troubles and the Civil War, in an Ireland that has entered the 'devil era'. Those were years characterized by reprisals and executions, and it is tempting to guess that some such event has struck into this Chapelizod family: that Anna Livia's last monologue, in short, is the rambling of a widow working to prolong her merciful sleep, the morning after the wake for a political victim who was her husband. He was of foreign (Scandinavian) origin; insofar as she is Ireland, this stranger has died for her. And now she addresses his shade with seductive confidence, torn between knowing he is safely dead and fearing to awake and know he is not there. Asleep, she fancies herself putting out his clothes and enticing him to go on a walk.

Here is your shirt, the day one, come back. The stock, your collar. Also your double brogues. A comforter as well. . . . Come and let us. We always said we'd. And go abroad. Rathgreany way perhaps (FW 620). . . .

Her wistfulness mixes his absence with his presence, buried hopes with future possibilities.

It seems so long ago, ages since. As if you had been long far away. Afartodays, afeartonights, and me as with you in thadark [40 days, 40 nights, the ark/the dark]. You will tell me some time if I can believe its all. You know where I am bringing you? You remember? . . . I could lead you there and I still by you in bed [she is still in bed, but not by him]. . . . Not a soul but ourselves. Time? We have loads on our hangs. [Hangs!].

As wakefulness floods toward her the struggle to stay narcotized takes a new turn; an available luxury is pitying herself, and the first stage of self-pity is the surrender of will: she becomes the river flowing out to sea. So she has rejected her husband – not been left widowed by him – and is on her way back home to her father.

A hundred cares, a tithe of troubles and is there one that understands me? One in a thousand of years of the nights? All me life I have been lived among them but now they are becoming lothed to me (FW 627). . . .

She is disappointed Cinderella, even:

I thought you were all glittering with the noblest of carriage. You're only a bumpkin. . . . Home! My people were not their sort out beyond there. . . . and weary I go back to you, my cold father, my cold mad father, my cold mad feary father (FW 628). . . .

If this book's end joins its beginning, that is because, from a nightmare of history exceeding anything dreamed of by Stephen Dedalus as long ago as 1904, there is no awakening, only an endlessness of killings, bombings, betrayings. That last speech of hers – of Cathleen ni Houlihan's – in one long evasion of him and of waking: evasion of simple unideolized realities no daughter of Eire any longer dares embrace. Many men have died for me, she will go on saying, many brave men, and she will let them think that she is a young girl still, with the walk of a queen. Reflecting on the unnerving way Joyce's women double and dissociate and lose their wits, we may discern in the women's dialogue of the James Joyce Repertory company, with always two female leads, his profoundest critique of the mythology of the revival.

THE DRAMATIC TREATMENT OF ROBERT EMMET AND SARAH CURRAN

MAUREEN S.G. HAWKINS

Robert Emmet has always had an importance in the Irish imagination far in excess of his actual contribution to Irish history. He was so popular with the people that Sean O'Faolain tells us a typical Irish home of his day would be furnished with 'pictures of Robert Emmet and Pius X on the walls',[1] while Robert Kee says that even 'constitutional opinion had . . . accepted Emmet as [a] legendary [hero]'.[2] Other rebels chose him for a role model: Pearse deliberately sited St. Enda's in the vicinity of the Priory, Sarah Curran's home, as he felt the location would 'inspire because of association with the exploits of the rebel Robert Emmet'.[3] Writers, too, found him an important source of inspiration: ballads were composed about him; Moore based some of his *Irish Melodies* on him and Sarah Curran; and even American writers, like Washington Irving, were captivated by their story. It is on the stage, however, that Emmet and Sarah have reigned most strongly. There have been over forty plays about Emmet; by writiers as well known as Dion Boucicault, Lennox Robinson, and Denis Johnston, as well as by writers never heard of before nor since. His story had been dramatized in German as well as in English, and set to music in two operas. These plays satisfied a number of needs in both the authors and their audiences; needs affecting the manner in which he was presented and often twisting him quite out of his historical character.

One of the strongest needs so served was that of defining 'Irishness'. Emmet was raised to the level of legend and, as Standish James O'Grady noted, 'legends represent the imagination of the country, they are that kind of history which a nation wishes to possess. They betray the ambition and ideals of the people.'[4] Emmet became the exemplar of true 'Irishness' as it was perceived by each author, and was often made a useful vehicle for propaganda. In the process he became everything from a Gaelic Leaguer to a Unionist. After the Civil War, Emmet was so accepted as embodying the Irish national image that plays about him came to be used to re-examine that image.

Before the Civil War, Emmet was, except in Digges's *Robert*

Emmet, presented as an ideal Irish patriotic hero, though the definition of these terms often changed from play to play. For Bannister and Pilgrim, the American authors of the first two Emmet plays, he is an 'Irishized' American with his roots in the stock hero of the American patriotic dramas Bannister usually wrote. The Englishman Digges's Emmet, on the other hand, looks on emigrating to America as a horrible exile and becomes a repentant Unionist by the end of the play. He is also, for the first time but not the last, portrayed as a Roman Catholic; clearly reflecting that Irish nationalism and Roman Catholicism had become synonymous.

Dion Boucicault's Emmet is also a Catholic, but, like Bannister's and Pilgrim's Emmets, he is a dedicated republican. While he favours Irish independence, he is not, like their Emmets, anti-English; Boucicault always had an eye on the British and Irish markets, even though this play was slated for American production. Accordingly, devotion to Emmet rather than to rebellion is the criterion for 'true Irishness'. Tynan's Emmet is also a republican, but here it is republicanism itself that is the touchstone of national identity. This Emmet, however, does add a new dimension to the composite portrait: he is the first Emmet to be identified with other Irish rebels and hence to become the type of the generic Irish patriot. Mangan's Emmet adds yet another layer to the image; his Emmet is a Gaelic League spokesman who lectures Napoleon, Thomas Russell, and anyone else who cannot escape, on the importance of the Irish language, on British cultural, linguistic, economic, religious, and military imperialism, and on the nature of Irish identity which, despite his insistence that anyone who is devoted to Gaelic League ideals is a 'true Irishman', seems nevertheless to presuppose a special position for Roman Catholicism and the native Irish-speakers of the West of Ireland.

Emmet has, to say the least, become a stock figure by this time, and authors such as Redmond, Connell, Robinson, Hepenstall and Kane use him as a yardstick to measure the patriotism and motivation of others. For the last two playwrights, he represents an ideal so institutionalized that his actual presence is not even required. His example is invoked by merely hanging his picture on the wall. Both Connell and Robinson treat him as a hero and use his story to examine the weaknesses of the Irish people, weaknesses which they see as having caused Emmet's revolt to fail. Robinson felt that the purpose of Irish drama should be to 'criticize ourselves ruthlessly'[5] and both writers use Emmet's story to do so from a strongly nationalist point of view. Mangan had followed history in making Emmet a Protestant, though he obviously felt it was more Irish to be Catholic, but Connell takes this Roman Catholic chauvinism one step further when the Catholic Kate expresses her surprise that Emmet is not, as she assumed, a Catholic too. This Emmet places himself firmly in the Anglo-Irish tradition from which he has sprung, and it is the newly emergent Catholic middle class who are here seen as undermining the cause of Irish independence through an avid West Britonism.

The Troubles, especially the Civil War, forced a re-evaluation of Emmet and of the cause he represented. As a result, Emmet could never again be treated uncritically as symbol and touchstone of the Irish identity, except in civic pageants like MacLiammóir's *Masque of Dublin* or MacMahon's *The Pageant of Pearse*. Fanning, while apparently not treating Emmet as such a symbol, is atavistically uncritical of him in *Melody Alone*. All the other post-Civil War playwrights tend to use him in one of three ways:

1) as a symbol of Irish nationalism and the physical force movement, through which to critically examine the effect of these forces on post-Civil War Ireland. This, the most common use, may be seen in plays like *The Old Lady Says 'No!'*.

2) Emmet may be used as an excuse to present a naturalistic examination of one or more of the subsidiary figures in his story; *Aaron, Thy Brother*, for example, concentrates on Sarah's father, John Philpott Curran.

3) Very rarely, as in Giltinan's *A Light in the Sky* or Iremonger's *Wrap up my Green Jacket*, a playwright attempts to present his understanding of Emmet, the man behind the legend, and of the forces which drove him, those same forces which later impelled all the Irish combatants between 1916 and 1923.

But what were the underlying foundations of this preoccupation with Emmet? One important aspect of the evolving myth is the theme of the blood-sacrifice: the idea that the hero's actions assume meaning from his death; that his insurrection is sanctified by his blood; and even that not dying would be a betrayal of his ideals, of the men he led and of Ireland herself. Belief in the necessity of the blood-sacrifice to redeem Ireland became increasingly widespread in the nineteenth century,[6] so much so that Yeats, in *Cathleen ni Houlihan*, could present 'such a sacrifice [as] . . . not merely . . . worthy of admiration, but actually advocated as the bounden duty of each Irish generation',[7] and Pearse could preach that 'the blood of the sons of Ireland [was needed] to redeem Ireland . . . a sacrifice Christ-like in its perfection . . . dying that the people may live, even as Christ died'.[8]

Emmet as Christ-figure is evident in many of the plays. Bannister and Pilgrim present him so, through his betrayal by his best friend, Kernan. Clarke carries the parallel even further: Emmet's friends desert him when they hear he is to be arrested; his betrayer hangs himself in remorse after his death. MacLiammoir's Emmet, too, has a Judas.

Though Emmet is early portrayed as a martyr, he is not treated as a self-conscious martyr until Boucicault's *Robert Emmet*, in which he rejects a pardon (pardons were *de rigueur* in the play tradition that Boucicault was working in), choosing death as preferable to denying his cause. Indeed, he believes that, should he deny it, that denial would cost him his 'life to come'[9] (and, considering the tableau that ends the play, it would appear he is right). Irish independence is God's cause, as it is in Johanna Redmond's *Falsely True*. Sacrifice is made an integral part of the rebel-hero's role – and that sacrifice must be the ultimate one. Thus it becomes his death rather than his military success, or lack of it, that marks the legitimate hero. Clarke agrees with this: in his *Robert Emmet*, Michael Dwyer points out that 'the shamrock grows better when there's dead men at the roots',[10] and Mangan's Emmet, also, accepts the need to water the shamrock with blood. Connell's Emmet, too, accepts it. Not only is he willing to become one of Liberty's doomed lovers; he idealizes those who have already died for her.

Robinson's Emmet is the first to reject the idea that the greatest thing a man can do for Ireland is to die for her; he would rather fight for her. Nonetheless, even Robinson cannot evade the force of this component of the Emmet myth; in the end Emmet dies because Ireland is 'more to him than life or love'.[11] The notion that Emmet might not have *wanted* to die gains adherents after the grim realities of the Civil War have undermined the romantic imagination of the period before it: Daveron tells Minnie Powell, in *The Shadow of a Gunman*, 'No man willingly dies for anything'.[12] It is only in pageants like MacLiammoir's that Emmet still deliberately, and with the author's approval, chooses to join 'those bands of martyred heroes who have shed their blood on the scaffold and in the field in defence of their country'.[13]

Despite increasing authorial disapproval, however, the theme of the blood sacrifice proves difficult to extirpate. *The Old Lady Says 'No!'* is a good example of this. Though Johnston attacks the Irish cult of death and martyrdom – first by satirizing Emmet's willing acceptance of it, then by forcing his Emmet to deal with death first-hand and find out how unromantic it is – the playwright cannot escape the necessity of turning Emmet into a Christ-figure, though not quite on the earlier model. His Emmet, too, must die to carry out his redemption of Ireland, though the emphasis is different: Emmet's creative act, rather than his death, acquires the redemptive focus.

Other post-Civil War writers have grappled with this sacrificial theme, but only Iremonger completely exorcises it in favour of life. In Craig's *Farewell, Companions*, MacNally bitterly comments that Emmet is quite willing to make a martyr of himself, yet the playwright's attitude towards Emmet as Christ-figure remains ambiguous. Giltinan, in *A Light in the Sky*, cannot quite escape the cult of the blood-sacrifice. Though his play is designed to reveal the human Emmet, the patriot's death-mask broods over the entire production and, in the end, the Actor concedes that there is, after all, nothing left of Emmet but 'a death mask . . . and a song'.[14] Though the author wants to escape the myth, society and the weight of tradition will not permit it. Even O'Donovan, who most bitterly satirizes the blood-sacrifice in *Copperfaced Jack*, is forced, if ironically, to admit its efficacy. Shanks, the Emmet-figure in the play, unable to realize his desire for power, claims himself willing, if not eager, 'to die for my country'.[15] Jack cynically eggs him on:

Death is *your* only hope, Peter. Die at the right time and a page of glory in the history books will be yours. . . . The only point in being a martyr is to be a martyr . . . When everyone's a martyr no one's a martyr. The only martyrs we remember are those who make themselves memorable. . . . History is short-sighted. You have to dance in front of her and wave your arms and shout to draw her attention.[16]

Shanks takes his advice and, sure enough, all the jailbirds who despised him become instant converts to his cult. The Warden's determination to hang his dead body, that the sentence may be carried out, of course links him to the men of the Easter Rising, especially Connolly; O'Donovan is making it quite clear that he does not limit his contempt of revolutionary heroes and the ethos of the blood-sacrifice to Emmet's case alone. Nevertheless, the traditional view persists in pageants such as MacMahon's *The Pageant of Pearse*, in which Emmet, a role-model for the young Pearse, is presented as having given 'himself without qualms or reservation'.[17] The cult of the dead hero has taken too strong a hold on the public imagination to be driven out; the most the iconoclasts cen do is attack it as they acknowledge it, while the more traditional writers still eulogize it.

But Copperfaced Jack's advice to Shanks as to how to win his place in history does not limit itself to advising him to die conspicuously; Jack also advises Shanks,

Have a lady in the case. Don't marry her, because there's no romance in marriage. Leave her, a lonely figure at the foot of your cross, to weep not for

Jerusalem but for you, and the sentimental bards will make us weep for you both.[18]

Although Sarah Curran is not present in all the Emmet plays, she is there in most of them, often playing a central role. Clearly she, or at least a female consort, is a significant part of the Emmet mythos. The earliest Emmet plays, those by Bannister and Pilgrim, have no Sarah; apparently the authors didn't know about her. But they do have a female consort for Emmet: Maria, who is Emmet's sweetheart in Bannister's play and his wife in Pilgrim's. She occupies the same place in these plays as Sarah does in the later ones.

Sarah, or her stand-in, is usually portrayed as totally devoted to Emmet and his cause; Bannister's Maria is a perfect example of this type. She supports Emmet's resolve, even though she fears for his safety and would like him to escape with her to America. Though she weakens briefly and urges flight, his refusal causes her to ask his pardon for her womanly weakness, and she sends him out to battle. Pilgrim's Maria, while behaving exactly the same, introduces another aspect of the treatment of the Sarah figure: she is, though innocent of any malevolent intent, the cause of Emmet's downfall; Kernan would not have betrayed the patriot had Emmet not won the woman he wanted. This, too, is the case with West Digges's Sarah Curran, even though in this play the informer wishes her hand only to use her father's and brother's influence to secure a government position. Nonetheless, he wants that so badly that he vows to be rid of his rival 'by a bullet or the halter'.[19] Clarke's Sarah also has a jealous suitor who betrays Emmet to the Authorities, but in this is encouraged by his evil cousin Malachi, who wishes to injure Sarah for personal reasons. Although Boucicault's Sarah doesn't have a frustrated suitor to betray Emmet, she is, despite supporting him and even saving his life by interposing her body between him and Major Sirr's gun, still the unwitting cause of his capture and death. He is betrayed by the follower he uses as lookout when he visits her, and it is at the priest's house, where he has gone to marry her, that he is captured. Tynan's Sarah has no treacherous suitor either but she, too, is the inadvertent cause of Emmet's destruction, as he trades his freedom for her life. This pattern of Sarah as loyal helpmeet and innocent cause of the hero's destruction is carried even further in Robinson's *The Dreamers*. His Sarah is an active rebel, yet Emmet again must allow himself to be captured to protect her. Carroll's Sarah, in *Death Closes All*, is of this type as well, though her devotion to Emmet is more personal and less political.[20] Yet, once again, she is the instrument of his destruction: her perfidious father betrays Emmet to protect his standing with the Castle government. Sarah, broken by being the cause of Emmet's downfall, goes mad, first demanding the head of her father on a plate and then rehearsing Emmet's trial in her mind.

Mangan's Sarah is the first to break this particular mould.[21] She opposes the rebellion and refuses to escape with Emmet, insisting on staying with her father, whose politics she defends despite his cruelty to her. Emmet, therefore, decides to stay too, to emulate her sense of duty. This Sarah is the first of a new type: Sarah as the culpable cause of Emmet's death. I believe this to be a basically puritan treatment, expressing the attitude of the nationalist who believes, as Boucicault's Emmet once said, that 'he who undertakes the business of a people should have none of his own'.[22] This puritan view is seen also in Fanning's Sarah.[23] Having declared her allegiance to Emmet's cause before the rebellion, she is all hesitation and vacillation after its failure, holding him just long enough for Major Sirr to find him. Michael Dwyer leaves her no doubt that she was Emmet's nemesis and, like Carroll's Sarah, she goes mad. Thus both are ruined – Sarah because she lacked faith, and Emmet because he allowed himself to be diverted to her from Cathleen ni Houlihan.

Craig's Sarah is also of this type. She doesn't want to share Emmet's dream; she only wants to marry him to escape her father, although when the rebellion fails she turns coy. When Emmet asks her to flee with him she replies, 'Ask me tomorrow, Robert, ask me tomorrow; a young girl must be asked twice'.[24] Emmet is taken because of her hesitancy, and she goes mad – with perhaps more justification than Fanning's Sarah, though it is hard to imagine this silly coquette caring enough about anyone to become so distraught.

It is Giltinan's Sarah, however, who is the epitome of the puritan view of Emmet's involvement with Sarah. While the author makes a serious attempt to portray Emmet as a human being, he fails to do the same for Sarah, though he portrays her as more deeply involved in the insurrection than any other author does. But she is a dangerous co-conspirator. She treats the conspiracy with all the childish glee of a twelve-year-old about to join a secret club. Her idea of the new order is of herself as 'the first lady in the land . . . consort of our country's liberator . . . receiving the guests . . . leading the ball . . . at Dublin Castle . . . [or] the Viceregal Lodge'; all Irish liberty means to her is the chance to become Dublin's leading social butterfly. She is vain, foolish, coy, flirtatious, and easily flattered; even into betraying Emmet's hiding-place. She has no common sense: she draws attention to Emmet's hiding place by visiting him, complete with coach, coachman, and her sister as chaperon. She sulks for days when Emmet reluctantly agrees with Anne Devlin, whom Sarah patronizes as her social inferior, that such visits are dangerous. She hides in the house, making Emmet come each night to her garden, until she decides to come out. As if this were not enough, she is the cause of his capture. Nor can she remain faithful to him. She sends him a letter the very day before the rebellion telling him that she is to marry another, a letter that spurs him to act rashly and so is yet one more way in which she dooms him. But then, this cannot matter much to her, since she appears to have been interested in Emmet only to escape her father, who jeers at her that she fancies herself as a 'romantic heroine'. If she does, however, it is hardly surprising, since Emmet has the same view and wonders, 'shall our names be linked together . . . yours and mine . . . Troilus and Cressida . . . Hero and Leander . . . Romeo and Juliet . . . will they set us in the firmament to move the hearts of future lovers?' And, in fact, that is how they are remembered, as the Caretaker makes clear by referring to Moore's song for her, 'She is Far from the Land', though he does speculate that Sarah's romantic broken heart 'must ha' been a bit rough on the poor husband', the British officer she married after Emmet's death.[25]

Farrington's Sarah is cast in the same mould, though she is weak rather than wilful, stupid and arrogant.[26] Her father, here presented far more favourably than elsewhere, asks if she will consent to be tried and jailed so that he can go on defending rebels, but she is frightened, so he gives up his cause. Sarah destroys his career by her attachment to Emmet, as she does in the plays by Carroll and Giltinan.

In only two plays is Sarah presented as opposed to Emmet's plans: Carroll's *The Conspirators* and Iremonger's *Wrap up my Green Jacket*. In each of them Emmet is treated as a symbol of Irish nationalism and the physical-force movement, both of which are portrayed as expressions of the cult of death and the blood-sacrifice. Sarah, representing the values of life and love, opposes him. In Carroll's play Emmet's fear that she might prefer a live lover to a dead hero has made him cold and hard to all human feeling. In Iremonger's verse play, Sarah wants Emmet alive and she resents the hegemony of the dead. She demands:

> Ireland talk to your dead! Tell we don't sleep at nights . . .
> Say this is a land for the living, the dead cannot claim it,
> Order them back to their serried graves, these phantoms,
> Who are disturbing constantly our short lives' ease and peace.

But Emmet, while in love with Sarah, 'love[s] a principle better than a girl'. It is only after he learns that she has gone mad that he feels remorse and returns to the human race.[27]

The Sarah figure in *Copperfaced Jack* is a departure from the usual portrayals of Sarah; Mary Neale is a street-smart sixteen-year-old who is willing to sell her body to save her life. Nonetheless, she's quite crushed that Shanks, the Emmet figure, refuses to marry her when Jack gives him the opportunity; Shanks, it seems, is unwilling to share the spotlight with anyone, even his beloved. Disillusioned with him and drawn to power, she turns to Jack for protection; ironically, fulfilling the prophecy that she, like the real Sarah, will 'marry afterwards – and . . . one of the hated oppressors'. But when Shanks' suicide and the stubborn insistence of the Warden on hanging his body win the rebel the public image he wanted, she, too, is drawn in and is left, 'a lonely figure at the foot of [his] cross'.[28]

But what of the other woman in Emmet's life, Cathleen ni Houlihan? Sometimes she appears in her own guise, sometimes in the guise of another, and, in some plays, in both. The first play in which she appears as herself is Digges's *Robert Emmet*, in which the 'Queen of Ireland', with a face in which 'all men may see a mother', visits Emmet in a dream. The bias of the play being Unionist, she can't very well console or encourage him, so she offers him a drink of whiskey, apparently the next best thing, and weakly says, 'I'm sorry you're leaving/The poor old country'. Honor, the cousin of Nora, the Sarah figure, and also in love with Emmet, appears as the earthly avatar of this queen; she even has the same face. Nora, herself, is also an avatar, thus completing a classical Celtic triad. Emmet tells us she is like the 'harp Heaven gave to Erin/ To tune all the hearts of the Emerald Isle'.[29]

Cathleen appears as herself at the end of Boucicault's play. Emmet, executed by a firing-squad, falls and

The wall behind [him] slowly opens. A vista of pale blue clouds appears. The figure of Ireland clothed in palest green and with a coronet of shamrocks in her hair descends slowly and bending forward when she reaches the spot behind Emmet, she kneels. Two children at her feet, R. and L., draw slowly back the body of Emmet until his head lies looking up into her face.

On earth, however, this goddess is incarnated in Sarah. Emmet regards the eve of his execution as 'the eve of my wedding night. I lie down in my grave to dream of [Sarah] until I wake to meet my bride at the alter of heaven.'[30] As we have seen, that bride proves to be Ireland herself. Sarah is not the only incarnation of Ireland in this play; Boucicault manages to personify every stratum of Irish society among her manifestations, thus legitimizing them all as 'real Irish' – at least as long as they are devoted to Emmet. Anne Devlin, Sarah's servant, is certainly so dedicated; she represents the peasant class and their devotion to Emmet. Tiney Wofe, Lord Kilwarden's daughter, also in love with Emmet, represents the upper-class Anglo-Irish. She performs the dual function of forgiving Emmet for Kilwarden's death – in her own person as Kilwarden's daughter and in her persona as an embodiment of Ireland – thus removing the only possible bar to his canonization. Cathleen ni Houlihan, therefore, in this play is a classically triune goddess, as she was in a rougher form in Digges's drama, and all three of her early aspects are subsumed in the Marian figure who receives the hero at the close of the play.

Cathleen ni Houlihan once more appears alone in her own right in MacLiammoir's masque, as the old woman who represents both Ireland and Dublin – an indication of the increased urbanization of Ireland. The Minstrel, echoing Yeats's description of his classic peasant Cathleen, prophesies, 'your daughter and your daughter's daughter will be in rags as beggars and in silks as a queen'.[31]

Johnston's Cathleen is also urban, but she is a much more frightening figure than MacLiammoir's, perhaps because, following the Civil War, she, as O'Casey says, appears 'very different . . . to the woman who used to play the harp an' sing, "Weep on, weep on, your hour is past", for she's a ragin' divil now, an' if you only look crooked at her you're sure of a punch in th' eye'.[32] No delicate maiden or venerable matron, she is a vicious harridan who demands blood and has no gratitude. Baulked by Emmet's refusal to yield her bloody due, she turns the crowd against him and thus uses him as the instrument to obtain her sacrifice from Joe. She loves none of her sons, neither 'the son that speaks . . . the son that swills . . . [nor] the son that dies', though the flattery of others will induce her to pretend such love. She is not the Sarah Emmet has been seeking, so it is particularly horrible to him when he realizes that she *is* Sarah, for Sarah and the Flower Lady are both aspects of Ireland. Yet it is only when he accepts this and accepts his own responsibility for her existence that he can, in a violent redemptive vision, affirm his rebellion, not for its physical aspects but for its metaphysical ones: the power of the dream and the Word and the Will; only thus can he redeem her, transforming Ireland into 'Paradise' where his 'Old Mother . . . will walk the streets . . . head high and unashamed'.[33]

Other writers use one or more of the characters to represent Cathleen ni Houlihan without presenting her directly. For Mangan and Giltinan, it is Anne Devlin who represents her; for Connell, it is Tom Moore's sister Kate, a social-climbing, name-dropping *arriviste*, eager to be thought genteel, and unanimous with her mother in declaring that 'no gentleman could be against the Government'.[34] Catholic Ireland has reached the middle class and likes it there; Kate would far rather flirt with Castle officers than succour Irish patriots.

The most common avatar of Cathleen, however, is Sarah. Even when Cathleen ni Houlihan appears in her own right, Sarah may still be an incarnation of her, as in Boucicault, Digges, and Johnston. Carroll's Sarah in *Death Closes All* may also be read as an avatar of the Goddess of Sovereignty of Ireland, though it is not necessary to do so. If one does, however, she presents Ireland as the traditional maiden in distress, here broken down by her father who has sold out to the British – himself, therefore, perhaps a symbol of the Ascendency who were bribed into passing the Act of Union. It might be thought hard to see Ireland in Fanning's Sarah, a weak, vacillating creature who brings about Emmet's capture. But her portrayal may be read in another light which makes Fanning's play, with its atypical treatment of Emmet for a post-Civil War play, fit its period more closely. Fanning's Emmet makes excuses both for Sarah and for the men who failed him; if Sarah is Cathleen, rather than Cathleen's rival, she is seen as having let him down badly and so fits all too well the post-Civil War image of Ireland and her treatment of her heroes.

O'Donovan's Sarah figure, Mary Neale, if examined closely also fits the post-Civil War image of Cathleen, even though she's a sixteen-year-old rather than a hag. Like Johnston's hag or the slut of Mrs. Galgoogley's come-all-ye, however, she is willing to sell her body to save herself; to accept a paternalistic British power, no matter how cruel; and to follow the scent of power. It is only when she recognizes the greater power inherent in the image of the dead rebel that she reaffirms her allegiance to him.

The only plays in which Sarah does not appear to be, in any sense, an avatar of Cathleen ni Houlihan are Carroll's *The Conspirators* and the plays by Iremonger, Craig, Giltinan, and, depending upon one's interpretation, Fanning. In these plays she is presented as the rival of Cathleen ni Houlihan, and in the last three plays Emmet's capture is treated as a punishment for his having succumbed to the unstable, coquettish, merely mortal charms of Sarah Curran when he should have devoted his life to the little old lady so that she might once again become the young beauty with the walk of a queen. In the first two plays, however, the authors reject the blood-sacrifice, and she becomes a symbol of life and love in opposition to death and patriotism.

In Carroll's *The Conspirators*, Cathleen is a composite figure much like that in the Flower Lady/Sarah in *The Old Lady Says 'No!')*. In *The Conspirators* Mrs. Galgoogly sings a come-all-ye that describes Cathleen as a prostitute to her conquerers, a drunkard, a pious hypocrite, and a poor mother to her children. Just as Sarah and the Flower Lady represent two aspects of that same Cathleen, so too do this Lady and Mrs. Galgoogley (a good mother who would 'tear out [her] eyes and give them to [her son] to see with . . . heart's blood to [him] to live with') represent the two sons of Cathleen.[35]

The oppositions between life and love, and death and rebellion, are more strongly presented in Iremonger's work; here they are not fused but at war with one another. Cathleen is 'Kitty Hooligan'[43] who wants blood as badly as ever the Flower Lady did. Sarah, for the first time, is her opposition, consciously and deliberately providing an alternative value system that finally leads Emmet to accept his own humanity.

If Sarah is an avatar of Cathleen – as, in whatever guise, she most often is – why should she almost always be the cause of Emmet's death? The answer to this, I believe, lies in the nature of Cathleen herself. Cathleen ni Houlihan is an aspect of the goddess of Sovereignty of Ireland and that goddess is, herself, an aspect of the Great Goddess, the goddess of life and death. She is both Demeter and Persephone, the mother of life above the earth and the bride of death below it. The Great Goddess always has a Son/Lover who is also the dying and reviving god, who dies for her and for his people, espousing her in the grave, and rising up from it that he may save them. The types of this couple have been many: Venus and Adonis, Ishtar and Tammuz, Mary and Christ; and, I submit, Cathleen ni Houlihan and her champion. If this is so and Sarah *is* an incarnation of Cathleen, Emmet *must* die since he is her lover; he must die *for* her and *because* of her, for in no other way can he wed her. Thus his cult must be a cult of blood-sacrifice, and his beloved must always be the cause of his death. Since the salvation he is to bring to Ireland is, in its origin, more mystical than political, his role as Ireland's champion is validated not by a successful rebellion but by his death for the land and the woman he loves – and these are ultimately synonymous. Several credible explanations have been given for the continuing popularity of the Emmet story, on stage as in poetry and ballad, but one of the deepest roots of that popularity may lie in an archetype, no longer consciously remembered – in an increasingly urban, English-speaking society – but still potent.

NOTES

1 Sean O'Faolain, *Vive Moi!* (Boston: Little, Brown & Co., 1964), p. 111.
2 Robert Kee, *The Green Flag* (London: Weidenfeld & Nicolson, 1972), p. 334.

3   Daniel J. O'Neill, 'Revolution, the Golden Age and the Irish', *A Review of Culture and Ideas*, V, 51 (June, 1976), p. 175.

4   Standish James O'Grady, *History of Ireland: Critical and Philosophical* (London, 1881), quoted in *1000 Years of Irish Prose*, ed. Vivian Mercier and David H.G. Greene (New York: Devin-Adair Co., 1952), p. 17.

5   Lennox Robinson, quoted in Harold Ferrar, *Denis Johnston's Irish Theatre* (Dublin: Dolmen, 1973), p. 17.

6   'Norreys Connell' [Conal O'Riordan], 'An Imaginary Conversation', *Shakespeare's End and Other Irish Plays* (Adelphi: Stephen Swift, 1912), p. 65.

7   David Blake Knox, 'Ideological Factors in Yeats's Early Drama', *Anglo-Irish Studies*, V, 1 (1975), p. 89.

8   Quoted, *Ibid.*

9   Dion Boucicault, 'Robert Emmet', *Forbidden Fruit and Other Plays*, ed. Allardyce Nicoll and F. Theodore Cloak (Princeton, N.J.: Princeton University Press, 1940), pp. 306–307.

10 Joseph Ignatius Constantine Clarke, *Robert Emmet: A Tragedy of Irish History* (New York: G.P. Putnam's Sons, 1881), p. 52.

11 Lennox Robinson, *The Dreamers* (Dublin: Maunsel, 1915), p. 72.

12 Sean O'Casey, 'The Shadow of a Gunman', *Collected Plays*, I (London: Macmillan, 1963), p. 109.

13 Michael MacLiammoir, 'The Ford of the Hurdles: A Masque of Dublin' (unpublished MS.), p. [60].

14 Donal Giltinan, 'A Light in the Sky' [original title: 'A Face in the Clay'] (unpublished MS.), p. 101.

15 John O'Donovan, 'Copperfaced Jack', *Seven Irish Plays: 1946–1964*, ed. Robert Hogan (Minneapolis: University of Minnesota Press, 1967), p. 257.

16 *Ibid.*, pp. 296–297.

17 Bryan MacMahon, 'The Pageant of Pearse' (unpublished MS.), p.12.

18 O'Donovan, p. 296.

19 West Digges, 'Emmet, or, The Harp of Erin' (British Library MS 53252A, Lord Chamberlain's Licence, No. 78), p. 7.

20 Paul Vincent Carroll, *Plays for My Children* (New York: Julian Messner, 1939).

21 Henry Connell Mangan, *Robert Emmet* (Dublin: Gill & Son, 1904).

22 Boucicault, p. 272.

23 J.I. Fanning, 'Melody Alone', *The Midland Tribune* (Birr, 1938?).

24 H.A.L. Craig, *Farewell, Companions*, music by William Alwyn (BBC, unpublished MS.), p. 101.

25 Giltinan, pp. 45, 100, 101.

26 Conor Anthony Farrington, *Aaron, Thy Brother* (Newark: Proscenium Press, 1975).

27 Valentin Iremonger, 'Wrap Up My Green Jacket', *The Bell*, XIV, 4 (July, 1947), pp. 11–12, 7.

28 O'Donovan, pp. 300, 297.

29 Digges, pp. 11, 85, 92.

30 Boucicault, pp. 313, 307.

31 MacLiammoir, p. [7].

32 O'Casey, pp. 131–132.

33 Denis Johnston, 'The Old Lady Says "No!" ', *The Dramatic Works of Denis Johnston*, I (Gerrards Cross: Colin Smythe, 1977), pp. 70, 74.

34 Connell, p. 71.

35 Paul Vincent Carroll, 'The Conspirators', *Irish Stories and Plays* (New York: Devin-Adair, 1958), p. 122. [Original title: 'The Loggerers'].

43 Iremonger, p. 27.

REWRITING HISTORY: ANNA PARNELL'S 'THE TALE OF A GREAT SHAM'

DANA HEARNE

The story of Irish women's participation in political life at one of the most momentous periods in Irish history caught my attention while I was writing a research paper on Charles Stewart Parnell, leader of the Irish Parliamentary Party from 1880 to 1891. This period all but encompasses the Irish Land War at its height between 1879 and 1882. It is also the period which sees the formation of the Ladies' Land League (1881), an unprecedented initiative in women's participation in public life in Ireland.

Reading the history surrounding Parnell over a period of approximately one hundred years, I was struck by the almost total absence of women from the record. One or two histories give them a passing and even partially favourable mention, while most histories either omit them entirely or tear them to shreds. A good example of the latter tendency appears in *Parnell* (1925) by St. John Ervine. Ervine informs us that when the Land League was suppressed after the No Rent Manifesto, 'Miss Parnell's band of harridans took its place' (p. 158). He observes that Anna Parnell was mad and that the Ladies Land League was 'infested with fanatics like her'. Reflecting on all this female lunacy, he comments, 'Irish women, when they take to politics, have a capacity for fanaticism which is almost inhuman' (p. 199).

So it was, until recently, that these women, and all the women who came after them, who took an active part in the public life of the nation, were destined to be ridiculed, eliminated or at best underestimated by male historians. We need not be unduly surprised by this, since it is an obvious and a general truth that history has been (until feminist historiographers took to the field) the narration and analysis of past events from a male perspective. Even those male historians to-day who choose to concentrate on women's place in history – an advance, no doubt, on previous indifference – cannot seem to write their histories in a non-sexist way. I do not for a moment regard the omission of women from history as a malicious conspiracy on the part of men, but rather as an inevitable philosophical bias based on centuries of excluding women from the

138

arena of power. (The few exceptional women who have had posi-
tions of power throughout history do not alter the general perception of women as being entirely marginal to the political process.)
Set alongside this observation is the ironic twist that women's
possible intrusion into the male world was considered a dangerous
threat. For men particularly, such an incursion into the male arena
threatened to turn the world upside down.

Today I want to concentrate on the Land League years, particularly from January 1881 to August 1882 – a period during which the
Ladies' Land League took a prominent part in Irish political life. I
want to look at the ways in which some important male historians
have distorted the purpose and contribution of the Ladies' Land
League. Given the inevitable distortion of male historiography, I
would suggest that initially it would be best to explore women's
experience by taking the material from the records of women themselves and by subjecting male versions of it to the closest scrutiny.

In dealing with the Ladies' Land League I simply want to look at
it as the start of the important movement of women's active
involvement in Irish political life, and I want to reclaim it as an
authentic and integrated part of Irish history. We have not lacked
male voices detailing the excitement and drama of those years of
upheaval and revolution, and describing the courage and spirit of
the male participants. But, in a historiography that spans a hundred
years, the women who ran the revolution for a period of six months,
while the Land League leaders were in jail, either got little or no
mention, or were slandered in the manner already described. To
read finally Anna Parnell's version of the story, as told in her
unpublished history, 'The Tale of a Great Sham', is not only an
exhilarating experience; it radically alters our perception of the
period.

Far from the lunatic extremist she has been made out to be, the
history reveals a woman of immense intellectual and organizational
ability, thoroughly practical in her assessments of Land League
policy and of the revolutionary potential of certain political
strategies. I cannot, obviously, go into great detail here, but let me
speak selectively of a number of issues raised by the manuscript.

When the land war began in 1879 it was the opinion of some of
the more radical members of the Land League executive, especially
Andrew Kettle, that a complete resistance to rent would force
England to accede to the Land League demands for a peasant
proprietary. Before Anna got involved in the movement she was
under the impression that this was in fact what the League was
advocating. She soon realized, however, that there was a double
message abroad, which said to the tenantry 'Resist rent' – until the

last possible moment. It was a policy that came to be known as 'Paying rent at the point of the bayonet'. What it amounted to, of course, was an injunction not to pay rent, coupled with the promise of being repaid out of Land League coffers for any eviction that might be incurred during the temporary non-payment of rent. That money was then to be used for any legal expenses that might arise, and also for food. What it usually ended up being used for was rent. So you had the anomalous situation of the Land League leaders urging rent-resistance and then paying the rent themselves; hardly a situation to bring about a revolution.

As Anna rightly remarked, neither the landlord nor the British government suffered as a result of this policy. The rhetoric was revolutionary and called down the forces of coercion, but the reality fell far short of the rhetoric. In Anna Parnell's history this is perhaps the major focus; hence the 'sham' of the title. Throughout the period of the Ladies' Land League, January 1881 to August 1882, Anna devoted her efforts and the efforts of her organization to putting into practice what the male leadership was preaching. It was for this – taking the Land League seriously, as Anna puts it – that she was labelled outrageous and extreme. When she allocated money to provide huts for those tenants evicted for refusing to pay rent, she was accused of squandering the Land League's resources. Yet when she calculated what it would cost to put into practice the sham policy of the male leaders, the sum was far in excess of the expenditure planned by the women. Obviously, the men had not worked out the consequences of their own sham policy, either financial or political. No historian who has read her manuscript can doubt the accuracy of Anna's analysis.

From the hallowed precincts of Kilmainham Jail, the male leaders suddenly turned into revolutionaries and issued, two and a half years too late, a 'No rent manifesto' – this time a real resistance to rent! Anna's critique of this manifesto exposes it for the hollow piece of political bombast that it is. Among the promises and exhortations contained in the manifesto were the following:

Pay no rents under any circumstances to your landlords until the government relinquishes the existing system of terrorism, and restores the constitutional rights of the people.
Against the passive resistance of an entire population, military power has no weapons.
Our exiled brothers in America may be relied on to contribute, if necessary, as many millions of money as they have contributed thousands to starve out landlordism and bring English tyranny to its knees.
If you are evicted you shall not suffer.

(Quoted in MS., pp. 151–153)

Anna criticized this manifesto for its exaggerated pose, and for promising far more than its authors could ever deliver. But by far the most injudicious feature of the entire manifesto she found to be the manner in which the financial aspects of the matter were treated: 'It read to me like nothing but the language of lunatics' (MS., p. 155). In her view, the language was directly calculated to cause extra trouble for those who had to administer the funds so lightheartedly spoken of.

It did not matter to them that they had incited the tenantry as far as words can, never to be satisfied with anything we could do for them. (MS., p. 156)

Referring to the manifesto's promise that those evicted would not suffer, she had this to say:

Only by adopting the system of providing a certain amount of shelter where victims were expected BEFORE they took place, from the beginning, would it have been possible to prevent the evicted suffering in a country destitute of house-room, and this time was not the beginning but the end. (MS., p. 154)

We find, then, that in this revolutionary situation the male leaders were inciting the peasantry to rebel by the strategy of resisting rent: only, however, to the point of eviction; at which point they should draw back. Meanwhile, the women were urging the peasantry to resist rent, and were taking practical steps to provide shelter to those evicted for so doing. For this, they, and not the men, would be blamed (by the men, of course) for distributing the Land League funds 'at an alarming rate'. A close colleague and great admirer of Charles Stewart Parnell, William O'Brien, explains that Parnell had to cut off the Ladies' Land League bank account because they would not curtail their spending as he had advised. He goes on to say that nobody appreciated more truly than Parnell their daring and unselfishness, and that it was his financial soul alone that saw any defect in their operations. This assessment is distorted in several ways, and I will allude to it again. For the moment I simply want to say that later evidence confirms that Parnell objected to the Ladies' Land League more specifically on the grounds that they were too revolutionary at a time when he was beginning to stand for a moderate line and for an alliance with the Liberal Party.

At one point in the manuscript Anna gives an outline of what she understood the purpose of her organization to be. But, first, I want to look at the version supplied by the instigator of the Ladies' Land League: Michael Davitt, revolutionary leader of the Land League. In an interview recorded by Michael Cashman in his *Life of*

Michael Davitt (1883), Davitt spoke of the two objectives envisaged in the formation of the Ladies' Land League: 1) It would be the medium for all kinds of charity, would support the evicted tenants, and relieve all cases of distress; 2) It would keep up a semblance of organization during the attempted repression which he saw was coming. 'The Ladies' Land League', Davitt continues, 'was thoroughly successful in both objects, and to them is due the credit of saving the Land League and banishing Forster from Ireland' (p. 23). He goes on to heap praise upon the women for their amazing system of record-keeping, and describes the rest of their work as involving the erection of huts for evicted tenants, the provision of money for legal assistance, and the organization of boys' clubs for the purpose of teaching the history of Ireland.

Cashman then asks him what the ladies did when the leaders were in Kilmainham, and Davitt responds:

They kept the organization alive – they went around the country making speeches and urging upon the people to pay no rent, and were preaching the Land League doctrines as they were never preached before. (*Life*, p. 233)

Davitt further observes that being jailed did not scare the women at all but only increased their numbers by leaps and bounds. However, he remarks:

When it came to arresting young ladies and locking them up in felons' cells, as was done with Miss O'Connor, the English people began to cry 'Halt'. They were ashamed of what was being done. Mr. Gladstone's government had gone to that point where change was impossible except such a change as would involve the abandonment of the whole policy. They had arrested all the men, but they could not arrest the women, because the people would not support them in any such measure. Consequently, they found it necessary to retreat, and Mr. Forster was forced to resign. The Land League had won the fight, and the finishing blow had been struck by the Ladies of Ireland. (*Life*, pp. 233-234)

There are a number of contradictions in this narrative. On the one hand, it implies that the women were pursuing an extremely revolutionary path, so much so that they were considered to be politically dangerous by the British Government and had to be suppressed. On the other hand, this fact is not considered to be related in any way to the final outcome or 'settlement'. Rather, Davitt ascribes the settlement to the moral indignation of the English people at the spectacle of ladies being treated in such a dishonourable manner. This requires further analysis, but for the moment I will simply say that, apart from its refusing to acknowledge the revolutionary power of the women, it is misleading, is innaccurate, and leaves out of account the wheeling and dealing that had gone on between Gladstone and Charles Stewart Parnell for months before the signing of the Kilmainham Treaty; wheeling and dealing, I might add, that had a lot to do with Gladstone's conviction that Parnell was the only person who could control the rising peasantry, who were becoming increasingly defiant as a result of the political strategy of the Ladies' Land League.

Cashman finally asks Davitt what the work of the Ladies' Land League is now, to which question Davitt replies:

Entirely charitable. When the leaders of the Land League were released, the political work was resumed by them, and the ladies contented themselves with doing that which was charitable. Politically they had accomplished their work, had accomplished it notably. (*Life*, p. 235)

We may say, in fairness to Davitt, that he might not have been aware of the extent to which he was distorting the facts. We do know, however, that he was fully aware of the deep antagonism felt by many members of the executive towards the women. In any event, his account is fairly representative of the most favourable accounts that history has afforded us of the Ladies' Land League until the appearance of T.W. Moody's 'Anna Parnell and the Land League' in *Hermathena* (1974), and Roy Foster's *Charles Stewart Parnell: The Man and His Family* (1976).

Set alongside Davitt's assessment of the purpose of the Ladies' Land League, Anna Parnell's version makes a striking contrast:

That the women might carry on the work after the men were imprisoned was the only reason given in Davitt's letter, and was the only one I ever heard. (MS., p. 120)

Her analysis of the women's political position as contrasted with that of the men, and of the ensuing difficulties caused by the profound difference between them, is revealing. Anna recalls that when the time came for the women to take up the struggle, they found that they had to undo or try to undo the greater part of what the men had done, and so substitute for it something very different – almost its exact opposite. It had occurred to her that the men hadn't made very adequate preparations for a rent strike, and she states that had she known that they never intended that there be one, she would never have had anything to do with them. The very first thing that Anna noticed on taking up the leadership position was the nearly wholesale condemnation by the men of the women's getting involved at all. Charles Stewart Parnell and Dillon were hotly opposed to it; Michael Davitt, William O'Brien, and Andrew Kettle were among the very small minority who supported the idea. Indeed, Kettle initially had been just as opposed to the proposal as Parnell and Dillon. However, when he met Anna Parnell, his reservations vanished: 'I found Anna Parnell had a better knowledge of the lights and shades of Irish peasant life, of the real economic conditions of the country, and of the social and political forces which had to be acted upon to work out the freedom of Ireland, than any person, man or woman, I have ever met'. Her knowledge, he says, 'was simple, masterful, and profound. Ignorance of the ethics of the real conditions in Ireland has, in my opinion, been the chief cause of the failure of all our movements, and our leaders in their efforts to work out the redemption of the country. Anna Parnell would have worked the Land League revolution to a better conclusion than her great brother.' And, according to Kettle, Parnell himself had recognized, 'My sister knows all about Irish politics. She is never at a loss and never mistaken in a judgement' (Laurence J. Kettle, ed. *Material for Victory* [1968].

The hostility increased as time went on, yet it became apparent to the women that the Land League could not be making the progress represented by the newspapers and the speakers at Land League meetings: the better-off tenants were not withholding rent when the poverty cases were evicted.

Anna was forcibly struck by the contradictory attitudes of the executive of the Land League. They continually spoke of 'charity' and 'relief' whenever they spoke of anything being done for the evicted tenants:

Once I asked how tenants could be expected not to pay their rents if they were not provided for afterwards, and received the astonishing answer that there 'was not a single tenant in Ireland who would not pay the rent if he could'. (MS., p. 129)

Apart from the fact that this extraordinary answer made a mockery of what the Land League had set itself up to be, the women actually found its assertion to be untrue, and felt that the Land League might have achieved a great success had it really intended what it preached. In Anna's view,

One estate that was not paying rent, but the people going into Land League houses when the evicting army arrived would have constituted a much more alarming object lesson to landlords than fifty estates paying rents 'at the point of a bayonet'. (MS., p. 129)

The women proceeded to implement the more revolutionary policy, but with only partial success. Anna observes:

It is a common situation for those who take service under weak heads to find themselves in; namely fighting for the enemy instead of fighting against him. (MS., p. 134)

In retrospect Anna felt that people with aims so radically different and incompatible as those of the Land League and the Ladies' Land League had 'no business in the same boat'. But even when it became clear that they ought to dissolve, it was not easy for them to do so, because of the obligations they had towards those tenants who were adopting their system. Their resolution to continue and their reasons for making that resolution are most interesting, and once again give us a sense of the women's political clarity.

Anna perceived that one fact was very clear amid all the uncertainty and doubt: the Land League policy could last only a short time, because it involved such a drain on their financial resources. When the inevitable change occurred, resistance to rent on a national basis either would cease or would have to be turned into a genuine resistance. Anna concludes:

Should the latter method become the official one whatever chance of success it might have would be enhanced by previous preparation, which we, unconsciously, had already begun. So to remain, and try to prepare for the inevitable moment when 'Paying at the point of the bayonet' must cease, was what we actually decided on doing, rightly or wrongly. (MS., p. 133)

Had the women realized the extent of the sell-out, Anne feels, they would have found the courage to dissolve; or they might have become a charitable organization. Anna herself could not have been part of such an organization: 'I had always taken the position that the Land League funds were for the purpose of aiding tenants not to pay their rents after the famine was over'.

In view of the fact that Anna Parnell's manuscript history of the period has not yet seen the light of day, we might justifiably ask whether the more recent accounts have finally restored her and the Ladies' Land League to a position of honour in Irish history as T.W. Moody suggests. Two accounts, already alluded to, are worthy of mention: one, by T.W. Moody in *Hermathena* (1974), entitled 'Anna Parnell and the Land League'; the other, R.F. Foster's *Charles Stewart Parnell: The Man and His Family* (1976). It can immediately be said that these treatments are an immense improvement on anything previously written, but they by no means do full justice to the facts. Moody's article continues to misrepresent the women in certain ways, so it might be well to hold off judgement until his definitive piece on the Ladies' Land League appears in print in his book on Michael Davitt. Foster, who has gone to enormous lengths to settle the issue, still falls short of complete success. An examination of his efforts provides some valuable insights into the danger of distortion inherent in the writing of history.

We have to contend no longer with the age-old description of the Ladies' Land League as a charitable organization; it is finally recognized, thanks to Anna's manuscript, as a revolutionary organization. Nevertheless, there continue to be several issues, even in Foster's account, which require further examination.

The first issue is related to the story of the dissolution of the Ladies' Land League. Foster outlines the work of the Ladies' Land League and draws our attention to the fact that their programme was an expensive one by its nature; 'a point to bear in mind', he tells us, 'when considering the later disbanding of the movement on the grounds of undue extravagance' (p. 265). Later he reverts to a seeming acceptance of the 'outline of how the L.L.L. came to be disbanded . . . attested to by many authorities'. That account tells us that 'Parnell, infuriated by the Ladies' extremism and financial extravagance, cut off their funds and the movement collapsed' (p. 276). Foster then goes on to give us Anna's version of the story, and does this, it might be added, with great care and accuracy. He continues, however, to leave the impression that the old story 'attested to by many authorities' is substantially true and that Anna's version is merely an elaboration on this established fact. In my view, Anna's version changes the substance of the story entirely, making it clear that it was the women who wanted to quit at the earliest possible opportunity after the men's release from Kilmainham. Anna saw the *rapprochement* with Gladstone as a complete betrayal. The women told the men at a meeting that they wanted to quit on the grounds that they were exhausted and that they found it 'morally impossible to go on working with the men'. The men tried very hard to persuade the women to relinquish their name but to continue doing the work as it would be directed by them. They failed so to persuade them.

The story, then, would have been more adequately analysed in terms of power, and in terms of the incompatibility of two groups with very different political aims and methods. When I speak of power in this context, I mean to recognize the stark fact that even if the women had wished to continue in active politics, they would only have been allowed to do so had they changed their political outlook to suit the new political moderation so recently adopted by the men – eventually, an explicit moderation. It was the men who had the power to decide what direction the movement would take. Real leadership had only been possible for the women while they held the stage alone.

Another important issue is what Foster speaks of as Anna Parnell's 'tendency to elitism which so often characterizes a dedicated revolutionary'. (p. 263) The issue is an extremely complex one, and Foster does not deal with it at all adequately. 'I only wish', he notes Anna as saying, 'the tenants would be as determined with the landlords as they were with us.' And he remarks, 'Certainly Anna's memoir is loud in its denunciation of the weak spirit of the tenants'. He adds, as an afterthought: 'But she seems to restrict this concept to their approach to paying rents'; and later concludes: 'When she wrote bitterly about the decline of Irish politics, the elitism of her own approach is finally and categorically stated' (pp. 268, 269, 282).

My own interpretation of the relevant passages in the manuscript is quite different from Foster's. As I see it, Anna's bitterest attacks are levelled at the chicanery of the most prominent Irish leaders: for the way they continuously misled the Irish people as to what was expected of them; and for causing, by their double-talk, a deep confusion in the minds of the tenantry as to the best method of carrying forward their demands. Anna consistently maintained that

the most essential condition for success was that the peasants themselves should wish it. That they didn't wish it very much is certain – but they might have if they had been induced to begin it and had perceived the possibility of success before them.

This is hardly a manifestation of the 'typical elitism' that Foster affirms. Besides, one should be wary of using such a term loosely, for what dynamic leadership could ever be fully excused of the charge? Elitism as a concept requires a more careful treatment if we are to adequately understand its meaning in relation to Anna Parnell, or indeed to any political figure or group.

Yet another problem is raised by Foster's continued use of the term 'characteristically extreme' to describe Anna's political behaviour. When she is not being extreme Foster has characterized her behaviour as 'unexpected'; perhaps a re-evaluation would not be amiss. To call her 'extreme' and 'elitist' is, in my view, simplistic, and tends to trivialize her activity. Neither do I feel that the terms can be applied indiscriminately to political strategy and to platform rhetoric. Foster talks of Anna's speeches growing more radical after the passing of the 1881 Land Act. But the rational spirit of the manuscript seems to be ignored when he observes,

At this stage of course, her brother's public utterances took a similar path – but with a weight of sophisticated political calculation behind the decision which does not apply in Anna's case. (Foster, p. 272)

The problem here lies not in any desire on the part of Foster to diminish Anna Parnell (though this is the effect) – indeed, his admiration for her is explicit throughout the chapter – but rather in his attempt to juxtapose two entirely different approaches to political action, and then to judge them by the same yardstick; viz., their appropriateness in the constitutional arena. It is not that Anna lacks 'sophisticated political calculation', it is that she chooses to stay outside the arena of Parliamentary politics, while her brother chooses to work within that system. Whether that decision, or the radical stand it implies, is naïve or politically astute is an entirely different question. Furthermore, Foster's assessment entirely overlooks the dialectical nature of the relationship between the constitutional politician and the revolutionary.

Given the painstaking critique of the men's politics which Anna undertook in the manuscript – her repudiation of their exaggerated promises and violent platform language, their inability to seize the opportune moment to take political advantage, and their incompetence in financial matters – we cannot but urge a reassessment of this kind of interpretation, which has especially bedevilled women throughout history and forced us out to the margins of social and political action.

Finally, let me repeat that Anna Parnell gives a very detailed account of the dissolution of the Ladies' Land League and goes to some trouble to make it clear that the dissolution was the unanimous wish of the Ladies' Land League executive. In spite of this, Foster expresses great surprise that Anna could have let go so easily and withdrawn from politics without a fight. He decides that the death of her sister Fanny is in fact the real reason for her disappearance from the political scene. After Fanny's death, he tells us, Anna suffered a breakdown, and by the time she recovered it was too late to re-establish her position. Apart from the fact that this implies that Anna's own account in the manuscript cannot be taken seriously, it altogether overlooks Anna's closing remarks on the status of women in politics – her recognition of women's complete powerlessness to bring about, on their own, any social change. She describes the character of Irish men as being at present incompatible with any great change for the better, and she continues:

I say 'Irish men', because whatever the relative values of men and women may be, it is certain that the former cannot be done without, when it is a question of altering the status of a country. If the men of that country have made up their minds that it shall not be done, the women cannot bring it about. (MS., p. 257)

It is this recognition of women's political powerlessness that will inform the feminist women of the next century. The demise of Anna Parnell and the Ladies' Land League will be cited frequently by the next generation of women as an example of the political vulnerability of women, who, lacking the political status of men, remain mere parasites on male strength and male weakness. This is the insight that will inspire the suffragists and, more specifically, the suffragettes to make women's demands a priority in their political agitation in the first decades of the twentieth century.

Appendix

A REPLY TO THE TOAST TO CANADA: CAIS INTERNATIONAL SEMINAR, 1981

MARGARET LAURENCE

Like many Canadians, I owe much to Ireland. Indeed, what I owe is my very existence, for had my great-grandparents on my mother's side not emigrated to Canada from County Tyrone around 1850, I would not be here at all. Chance meetings and marriages, of course, determine the individual forms of *all* people, but apart from our native peoples who were here *first* and *foremost*, Canadians born in this country owe our own individual lives to the fact that our ancestors came here from somewhere else.

It always annoys me when I hear people refer to *English Canada*, meaning everything outside of Quebec. I realize that 'anglophone' is a rather clumsy term, but it is nonetheless the one I prefer, because, although not totally accurate, it is much *more* accurate than 'English Canada'. My own background, as it happens, like that of many Canadians, is not English. Mine is Celtic. My people on my father's side were Scots; on my mother's side, Irish.

When I think of our Canadian culture, our writers, composers and artists of all kinds, I marvel at the diversity of backgrounds – native Canadian Indian and Inuit, French, English, Irish, Scots, Jewish, Ukranian, Icelandic, Japanese, German, Chinese, Italian and many many more. I believe that this diversity, this variety, has added richly to our culture, as has the wonderful variety of our geographical regions. My prayer for Canada is that we may learn to value more greatly the multi-faceted nature of our land and our heritage, and to respect more greatly our differences.

It seems appropriate that this conference on *Woman in Irish Legend, Life and Literature* has taken place in this area, which was settled by so many tough-spirited Irish women and men who came to this land bringing their few material possessions and those other unseen and powerful possessions – their hopes, their need for freedom, their songs of lament and mourning, and their music of celebration and joy.

For myself, as a woman writer, I have always acknowledged my great debt to my mother and her three sisters, my aunts, one of whom became my beloved step-mother when my own mother died

150

when I was four. Those strong, intelligent women, who were devoted, respectively, to music, to the teaching of literature, and to nursing, the healing art, did, I believe, owe some of their qualities to their Irish foremothers.

It is, therefore, as Chancellor of Trent University, as a writer and as a woman, as a citizen of this area, and as a third-generation Canadian of half-Irish descent, that I respond with gratitude and thanks to the Toast to my country, Canada.

NOTES ON THE CONTRIBUTORS

LORNA REYNOLDS, formerly Professor of English at University College, Galway, has written extensively on many aspects of Anglo-Irish literature. She is joint general editor of the *Yeats Studies* series.

MAIRE CRUISE O'BRIEN has published three books of verse in Gaelic; together with literary criticism and other materials in various collections and periodicals. As a member of the Irish Foreign Service, she served in France and Spain and at the United Nations. She is joint author (with her husband, Conor Cruise O'Brien) of *A Concise History of Ireland*.

ANDREW PARKIN teaches English at the University of British Columbia. Author of several articles on Anglo-Irish literature, he has edited *Stage I: A Canadian Scene Book*, currently edits the *Canadian Journal of Irish Studies*, and is the author of *The Dramatic Imagination of W.B. Yeats*.

ANN SADDLEMYER, a Canadian by birth, and a Fellow of the Royal Society of Canada, is Professor of English and Drama at the University of Toronto. She has edited Synge's plays and written extensively about Synge, Yeats, Lady Gregory, and other modern dramatists. She is co-editor of a new journal, *Theatre History in Canada/ Histoire du Théatre au Canada*, and has recently published *Theatre Business*, an edition of the letters of the first Abbey Theatre directors.

J. PERCY SMITH, former Vice-President (Academic) of the University of Guelph, is author of *The Unrepentant Pilgrim: A Study of the Development of George Bernard Shaw* and of numerous articles on literature and on university government. He recently edited *Candida* and *How He Lied to Her Husband* for the Facsimile Edition of Shaw's plays, and is preparing another critical study of Shaw.

RONALD AYLING teaches at the University of Alberta. His many publications on O'Casey include *Sean O'Casey: A Bibliography* (with Michael J. Durkan), an edition of O'Casey's *Blasts and Benedictions*, and a collection of O'Casey criticism, *Sean O'Casey*, in the Modern Judgements Series.

HUGH KENNER, a native of Peterborough, Ontario, is Andrew Mellon Professor of the Humanities at the Johns Hopkins University, Baltimore. A versatile scholar and a prolific publisher, he is especially renowned for his work on Joyce.

MAUREEN S.G. HAWKINS, a post-graduate student in English at the University of Toronto, teaches English at Fourah Bay College, University of Sierra Leone, Freetown.

DANA HEARNE, a native of Ireland, who teaches at Concordia University, Montreal, is completing work towards a Ph.D. Degree, in the Social and Political Thought Programme, at York University, Toronto.

MARGARET LAURENCE, Chancellor of Trent University, Peterborough, Ontario, and a Companion of the Order of Canada, is an award-winning novelist of international repute. Among her most popular works are *The Stone Angel, A Jest of God*, and *The Diviners*.

S.F. GALLAGHER, Senior Tutor of Julian Blackburn College, and Professor of English Literature at Trent University, teaches Shakespeare, eighteenth-century literature, Shaw, and modern drama. He is preparing for publication a selection of plays by Hugh Leonard.

INDEX